THE COMPLETE
DIVORCE
RECOVERY
HANDBOOK

LIFELINES FOR RECOVERY SERIES

Zondervan's **Lifelines for Recovery** Series emphasizes healthy, step-by-step approaches for dealing with specific critical issues.

THE COMPLETE
DIVORCE
RECOVERY
HANDBOOK

A revised edition of *Second Chapter*

JOHN P. SPLINTER

ZondervanPublishingHouse
Grand Rapids, Michigan

A Division of HarperCollinsPublishers

The Complete Divorce Recovery Handbook
Copyright © 1992 by John P. Splinter

Requests for information should be addressed to:
Zondervan Publishing House
Grand Rapids, Michigan 49530

Library of Congress Cataloging-in-Publication Data

Splinter, John P.
    The complete divorce recovery handbook : grief, stress, guilt,
children, co-dependence, self-esteem, dating, remarriage / John P.
Splinter
      p. cm.
    ISBN 0-310-57391-2 (paper)
    1. Divorce—United States—Psychological aspects. 2. Divorced
persons—United States—Psychology. 3. Divorce—Religious aspects
    Christianity. I. Title.
    HQ834.S7 1992
    306.89—dc20   91–40785
                                               CIP

Edited by Evelyn Bence
Cover designed by Jack Rogers

Printed in the United States of America

98 99 00 01 02 03 04 /DC/ 10 9 8

To
Mike Cummings
Jack Easterling
Roger Hall
Sydney Jumper
Jan Miller
Lee Pflueger
Shelia Riddick

Without their input, research, editing (and reediting), and willingness to share personal experiences, there would be no book.

CONTENTS

PREFACE

In 1984, as director of what was to become a large and diverse ministry to single adults at Central Presbyterian Church in St. Louis, Missouri, I saw that my responsibility included helping people recover from divorce.

But what did it mean to "recover" from such a trauma? What help was needed? Looking for answers, I formed a committee of highly educated divorced people. Together we surveyed the existing divorce-recovery market. Was there a product that could meet our needs? While we found many short-term divorce-recovery programs, from an intense weekend approach to a six-week study, we knew that the recovery process could drag on, sometimes for years.

As we conducted our research, we discovered a doctoral dissertation that called for a divorce-recovery approach lasting fourteen weeks or longer. This observation concurred with ours. We also knew that the best healing would be effected within a small group.

That's how the *Second Chapter* project was born. We determined to write a book and build a ministry for divorcing people. Basing the ministry on the book, we would use our church as a base for the subsequent small-group ministry.

We found a publisher, and we were off and running. Four years later, having run the program ourselves and finding many other churches using *Second Chapter*, we decided to rework the project. How could we make it even better?

To bring you *The Complete Divorce Recovery Handbook*, we essentially tore the old project apart and began from scratch. We decided to modify the format so the book could be used as a self-help guide, easy to use by individuals whether or not they were involved in a divorce-recovery group.

Our team has put countless hours of research, editing, and creative input into this project. As was the case for the previous book, all but one person on the committee has been divorced. Everything in these pages has faced the harsh light of reality as seen through the eyes of people who know what it's like. Since these people have also led divorce-recovery groups for years, they know just what divorce recovery is all about.

The book is written with an eye toward both clinical and theological issues. Experience has shown us that one cannot effectively heal without addressing both the psychological (emotional-relational) and spiritual (God-related) issues inherent in the process of divorce and recovery.

This book represents a decidedly Christian viewpoint. Don't be surprised or offended to discover themes such as Scripture reading, prayer, and reconciliation to God. Yet the book makes no attempt to manipulate a person into a religious conversion.

We see that one's personal walk with Jesus Christ is a core issue in every aspect of living and healing. We say *a* core issue rather than *the* core issue, since many people in the throes of divorce already have a solid faith in and walk with Christ. For these, key issues may be codependency, dysfunctional family systems, clinical problems, uncontrollable choices made by a spouse, and so forth.

If you find yourself disagreeing with portions of this book, whether your disagreement is clinical or theological in nature, you might use the book as a starting place for discussion; weave your own thoughts or theological perspectives into the teaching and healing process.

‡

ACKNOWLEDGMENTS

It would be inappropriate for me to claim to be the sole author of this book. I must thank the first project committee: Jack Easterling, Sydney Jumper, Jan Miller, and Lee Pflueger. I also thank those who helped tear apart the original work and rebuild it. Jan Miller (project manager), Mike Cummings, Roger Hall, Shelia Riddick, and Bill Southworth. I am humbled to be surrounded and supported by such capable and loving people. Without you there would be no project. I have merely been the scribe, putting your thoughts and experiences onto paper.

Finally, I thank all those who have read and used *Second Chapter* and made suggestions for improving the program. We trust you will find this new work better in every way. This is not a simple republication of that work, but a thoughtful and thorough attempt at making this the most complete and helpful divorce-recovery resource available, written from a Christian perspective.

‡

HOW TO USE
THIS BOOK

This is not just another book about divorce recovery. It's intended to be used as a tool—requiring the involvement of the reader. If you just read the book and then put it on a shelf, the benefits will be minimal.

We easily identify three audiences for this book. Some individuals will be looking for relief from the pain of divorce. Others will be using this book as a course "text book." Still others will read from a more detached perspective, perhaps as a therapist or clergy, wishing to gain more knowledge about the subject of divorce.

IF YOU'RE GOING THROUGH DIVORCE
AND READING ALONE

Have a notebook handy. Read each chapter thoroughly. Underline. Make notes. Don't skim. Go for depth. Measure the book against your own experience. Think. Reflect. When you get to "Questions for Reflection," write thorough answers in your notebook. As you do so, you'll probably feel yourself progressing toward wholeness. We suggest you take a chapter a week, but set your own pace.

At the end of each chapter there is an "Action Items" section. Complete every action item, as each has a purpose—to challenge and stretch you toward healing. Again, keep a written log of your progress—your thoughts and feelings as you act, reflect, and pray.

The "For Spiritual Growth" section at the end of each chapter is aptly titled. Though you don't have to try to connect with God as you go through this material, hundreds of people who have used this book will tell you that divorce recovery is at least partially a spiritual journey; the closer one's walk with God, the more effective and deep one's healing. You decide how to handle the spiritual issue.

At the end of the book there is a comprehensive additional-reading list, in the event that you wish to read more about any chapter topic.

A DIVORCE-RECOVERY PROGRAM

Great idea. We usually heal better when doing so with the emotional support of other people. Use your divorce-recovery group as one place (among many) to learn once again to trust and connect.

If you're in a group, we suggest you meet weekly for at least two hours, taking one chapter per week as the basis for group discussion. Read the chapter during the week. Make notes. Complete the action items. (Read and follow the above suggestions for individual readers.) Then, as a group, discuss the issues presented in the chapter. We suggest you allot 20 percent of your time to the chapter text, 60 percent to the questions for reflection, and 20 percent to the action items. You may want to begin and close with prayer.

Group leaders should have gone through a divorce and be at least two years away from their date of divorce. (They may be remarried or not.) People who have not been divorced don't really know what it's like and people who are too close to their own divorce are usually too emotionally tied up in their own pain to be helpful to others.

Groups should include both sexes and be limited to ten participants, with two leaders per group (one man and one woman). More than ten (twelve including leaders) becomes a problem, as people "get lost" in the crowd. On the other hand, a group of fewer than four (six including leaders) can feel intimidating.

Leaders will want to provide a "safe" environment for participants. That means safety from intrusion into the group by a nonmember at any time, safety from disclosure of private information, safety from prying questions. The group should be a place where each member feels a protective "fence" around the group, a place where sharing is encouraged, where aching hearts are protected and nourished. We don't recommend meeting in homes, especially if children of any age might barge in.

Groups must be *closed*. That is, once they are formed and have met once or twice, newcomers or visitors should not be permitted. One of the objectives of divorce recovery is to reestablish trust—which is difficult enough in the company of familiar faces without having to struggle with outsiders dropping in. For group members, regular attendance should be required. You'll want to make this easy by establishing a regular meeting place and time. A more complete leader's guide for a divorce-recovery group is available from *Second Chapter*, 7700 Davis Drive, Clayton, MO 63105.

Anyone using this book as a basis for a small-group divorce-recovery program should clearly understand and live by the following ground rules.

GROUP GROUND RULES

Personal Conduct

1. Don't analyze, probe, push, or evaluate one another.
   a. Don't attempt to analyze or interpret the motives of another group member (e.g., "I think the real reason you stopped loving your spouse was because of the affair you were having").

   b. Avoid probing into the privacy of another member (e.g., "So what happened on your last date?" "Why doesn't your kid like you?").

   c. Avoid pushing people to share things they'd rather keep confidential (e.g., "You always clam up when we talk about sexuality. What's the matter with you?").

   d. Avoid evaluating or passing judgment on the statements, feelings, or actions of another group member (e.g., "You really were a jerk! I can't believe you did that! No wonder he left you!").

2. Don't give unsolicited advice (e.g., "Well, if I were you, in this situation, I'd put sand in her gas tank").

3. Limit your advice to:

   a. your own personal experience, fully realizing that your experience may not be applicable for another person;

   b. your own feelings about the situation, (e.g., "When I hear you say that I feel angry—sad, etc.").

4. Respect your group leaders. They are here to guide your healing process. Whether or not they are professionals, they are in a position of leadership. Your help in supporting them will be necessary and appreciated.

Group Conduct

1. Keep absolute confidentiality with no exceptions. Healing will proceed more quickly when group members feel safe to share their most private pain. Nobody has the right to compound the pain of another group member by telling others things shared in confidence within the group. Members taking group information outside the group will be asked to leave the group.

2. Be responsible to your group.

   a. Be punctual, courteous, committed, and willing to work together. Everyone is important; nobody is more important than anyone else.

   b. Don't dominate the group, but don't "hide out" either. If you hear your voice too much (or are getting cues from others that you're talking too much), try to stop and listen. If you don't talk much at all, try to share more openly.

3. Don't date group members.

   a. Protect yourself against getting so intimate with one of your group that you ruin your ability to participate with the group. You've got enough to tend to at this time without falling in love with another wounded person.

   b. Protect the group. Avoid any one-on-one encounters of any kind with group members of the opposite sex. Whether it's a date or just going out for coffee, for the time being, *don't*. If you want to talk privately with someone, call one of the group leaders or a group member of your own sex. Remember that *everyone* in the group is vulnerable right now. One-on-one relationships with group members of the opposite sex risk slowing down (or stopping) the other person's healing as well as your own. It will also be destructive to the group process.

4. Keep divorce-recovery work for the divorce-recovery group. If you're out with a few members of your group, don't use that time for intense, therapeutic conversation. For successful group work, you should have a neutral and trained third party, such as a group leader or a therapist. Without such leadership you risk doing damage to one another.

IF YOU'RE A PROFESSIONAL

This book is an attempt at blending both clinical and spiritual data, aimed at healing mind and spirit.

If you're a therapist, you'll find this book clinically eclectic. It's not based exclusively on the psychodynamic model, family systems, behaviorism, or any of the cognitive models; it includes pieces of each. Most of the technical language one might find in purely clinical texts is expressed in terms the lay reader would understand. Though written initially for the lay person to use as a self-healing tool, it has been found useful by many clinical professionals.

If you're a pastor, note that the book is not written from a specific theological perspective. It is not intended to be an apologetic for any specific denomination or theological position. Yet Scripture is referenced at the end of each chapter. It is woven into several chapters, and chapter 10 deals specifically with biblical insight regarding divorce and remarriage.

‡

CHAPTER 1

GOOD GRIEF

I am weary with my sighing; every night I make my bed swim.
Psalm 6:6 (NASB)

It was a loss, a major loss, Even though it was almost inevitable, when it happened it was a loss, and it ached.

Some describe it as heavy sorrow, others as deep sadness. However it is described, grief is a monumental, wearying, and sometimes devastating emotional process.

Grief is caused by some kind of loss, usually of a loved one, as in the case of death or divorce, but sometimes the loss involves a job or a home or something more vague, such as community respect or position. Grief is a normal reaction to a painful situation and is one of the most deeply disturbing emotional states a person will ever endure. It is usually an inescapable part of divorce, as two people tear apart what had once been a bonded, close, significant, intimate relationship. But it's more complicated than that. While divorce may symbolize the death of a relationship, the relationship is not really dead, especially when there are children involved.

Funeral services are helpful for people grieving the dead because they provide a mechanism whereby the mourner can understand that the relationship is absolutely and forever terminated. Since there are no funeral services for divorce, grieving can become a prolonged and complicated process. Although the relationship is legally terminated, it frequently is maintained in some crippled form.

Though I say a divorce is not as final as a funeral, let me point out that there is a real difference between being separated and divorced—even if the separation lasts three years, even if the marriage died ten years ago. As Yogi Berra once said, "It ain't over till it's over."

The day of divorce does one thing, if nothing else: It begins the process of putting back together the lives of both parties—in a new form. On the day of divorce, some questions are answered: One learns what financial settlement will be granted. As a result of this financial knowledge, one knows what kind of housing one will be able to afford. One learns who will get primary custody of the children, and what rights of visitation will be granted.

Few if any divorcing people think that their attorney did as good a job for them as they had hoped. Still, now that the gavel has dropped and the judge has issued the edict legally terminating the marriage, there is a more recognizable future, things are a little more certain and under control.

Again, the day of divorce doesn't represent a final point in anything but the legal status of the marriage. For many, ongoing battles will continue for months or years.

Not everyone will walk through the grieving process in the same way. Each person comes equipped with a unique style, personality strength, level of support from others, level of self-esteem, level of personal insight, personal flexibility, spiritual depth, and so on.

Though every person's grieving process is unique, there is a relatively predictable cycle of feelings. And eventually the cycle ends. That is, if you're in the midst of the worst and wildest emotional roller coaster ride you can imagine, know that you will one day be normal again.

This does not mean that your feelings will be "boxed" and predictable or even logical. At one moment you may feel desperate hopelessness, sadness, and loneliness. Two hours later you may feel deep anger, bitterness, and hatred. That night you become overwhelmed with fear, even terror, then relative calm and normalcy. Feelings fluctuate a great deal, from high to low, from low to lower. Yet grief generally follows a progressive pattern. Understanding this pattern can give you a hopeful perspective: No stage lasts forever.

SHOCK

Grieving frequently begins with an overwhelming shock, a stage of disbelief, horror, and numbness. "What? This is happening to me? How could it be? Surely I'll wake up in the morning and find out it's just been a bad dream. Won't I?"

The stage of shock provides some emotional padding that temporarily shields one from the deep trauma of the loss causing the grief. It provides temporary emotional distance, allowing one's vision to slowly focus on the reality at hand. The mind puts the events "on hold," keeping reality at bay.

Not everyone going through divorce faces shock. In some cases the real shock occurred several years before, when it became apparent that the marriage was terminally ill. In some cases the shock resulted from physical abuse or knowledge of a spousal affair. In other cases a spouse may have withdrawn deeply in response to angry words. There is often a deepening sense of marital failure and an increasing knowledge that divorce is imminent. Spouses usually do not face the shock of separation and divorce simultaneously. When the actual divorce is underway, one partner is usually more traumatized than the other.

The spouse who left the marriage—dump-er—is usually further ahead in the grief process, having made some very serious decisions some time before the other party may have even known that divorce was being contemplated. The dump-er may have gone through the stages of grief months or even years before.

The dump-ee might be struggling with shock and anger when the dump-er is entering the stage of acceptance. This can cause problems, as the dump-ee looks at the dump-er and assumes, "That jerk isn't hurting at all!"

It's a futile guessing game to figure out who hurts more during a divorce. Frequently the pain of both partners hits on a different curve, at different times, and sometimes even for different reasons, all of which can make it appear as if the other person is either a nonfeeling droid or a kookie emotional case.

DENIAL

Sometimes the stage of shock is skipped or delayed, and someone facing a loss shifts right into the stage of denial. Denial can be an extension of shock, but there's a subtle difference: In moving from shock to denial, one moves from "This can't be happening to me," to "This *won't* happen to me," or "I won't *let* this happen to me."

In denial one actively "pretends" a loss isn't going to happen. The person goes on with life as if everything's normal. A person in denial is safe from much of the pain that lies outside denial and most often completely unaware that he or she is living in denial (to the point that he or she may think that everyone else is crazy for not seeing the situation as it is). If a husband files for divorce, and the wife immediately leaves town thinking the action will somehow prevent the divorce, she's likely living in denial.

In divorce the stage of denial may include lengthy court battles and postponements or refusal to cooperate in the legal process.

Self-pity is frequently a form of denial. "Poor me! I never deserved this! He/she was such a *#@**#@!! I can't believe he/she did this to me. How could I have married such a selfish jerk! I think that all men/women are jerks! And now what are the children going to do? Woe is me!!"

If one can work one's self up to a sad enough frenzy of self-pity, then one doesn't have to face the reality of divorce or accept the pain of it. This technique is like knocking out a tooth on the left side of the mouth so that the one on the right side won't hurt quite as badly.

Self-pity can include wallowing in remorse or regret, focusing on old anniversaries, and spending (way too much) time reminding one's self (and others) of things that meant a great deal within the marriage.

ANGER

As denial can be an extension of shock, anger can be an extension of denial. The two stages frequently overlap. When a family splits apart, anger, hatred, and rage can be frighteningly deep. This deep anger can be productive or destructive—depending upon how it is managed.

Anger must be faced and managed. The fact is that anger *will* be handled, in one way or another. If you don't control it and use it for your growth, it will control you. Unexpressed or unresolved anger is one of the primary, perhaps *the* primary, source of clinical depression.

Religious people often have difficulty resolving their anger because they mistakenly believe that their faith does not allow for its expression. Consequently they internalize it, denying that it exists or turning it into thinly disguised, covert, nasty actions and/or words. Either way, a volcano will eventually erupt.

The eruption may be external (screaming, bashing things, dragging an ex-spouse back to court, overdisciplining the children, being a tyrant at work, and so forth) or internal (ulcers, heart attack, migraine headaches, menstrual problems, high blood pressure, colitis, depression). It becomes apparent that internalized anger is not resolved anger.

Reflect for a moment on the fact that God created us as emotional beings. In several situations, Christ himself expressed anger. He was often angry with the Pharisees. He once made a whip of cords and chased people out of the temple. In the Old Testament God was frequently angry with Israel, to the point of telling Moses that he intended to destroy the nation.

Despite what some say, there is no difference between righteous and unrighteous anger. Anger is anger. Period. What one chooses to *do* about the anger may be righteous or unrighteous, but anger is a legitimate, God-given feeling, a signal of fear or sadness.

In Ephesians 4:26 Paul says, "BE ANGRY, and do not sin" (NKJV). That is, if you are angry, recognize the emotion for what it is. Express your anger, but in a way that will not cause you to sin. It is not wrong to say to somebody, "I'm angry." It *is* wrong to express the feeling by smashing a baseball bat into your ex-spouse's windshield.

How is acting out one's anger destructive? Say a man aims his anger toward his wife, calling her names, slashing her tires, harassing her with telephone calls. Or a wife aims her anger at her husband, sending poison-pen letters, calling and hanging up at 3 A.M., pouring sugar into his gas tank. These examples of anger management are destructive in at least two ways: (a) They cause the targeted person to become defensive, escalating the conflict. (b) They cause the angry person to become increasingly sneaky, manipulative, vindictive, hostile, and punitive.

Again, one doesn't have to admit anger to act it out. This is often seen when the children become pawns in an ugly game. A man who claims he's not angry with his ex-wife may withhold child support checks. In turn, she withholds child visitation from him. She may say that she's not angry with her ex, but her words are overruled by her actions. (Incidentally, if in doubt, believe actions before you believe words. Noted psychologist Hiam Ginott is quoted as having said that a person can act nicer than he feels—but not much.) In the end, the kids pay the price for this form of anger management, learning not to trust either parent and becoming isolated from any source of love.

Some people use mutual friends as pawns in their angry game—getting them to take sides, to spy on or pressure an ex-spouse. Always remember this: A bond of hatred is just as strong as a bond of love. It just hurts more.

It is possible to *remain connected* to an ex-spouse via a prolonged and angry relationship (during separation or even after divorce) within which one uses every possible form of social relationship to damage the ex-spouse. It's still a connection, and for the desperate person, even a horribly bad, painful connection is sometimes better than no connection.

But anger acted out (directly or indirectly) toward the spouse will only intensify the battle and the pain. Nobody wins. Everyone loses.

How does one productively resolve anger? Here are some suggestions:

1. Don't deny your anger. Recognize it. Let it exist. Even God gets angry, so why can't you? (See Exod. 4:14; Num. 11:10; Deut. 29:23; Josh. 7:1; Judg. 2:14; 2 Sam. 6:7; Eph. 4:26).
2. Admit it to yourself. Say it out loud. "I am angry. In fact, I'm more than just angry. I'm hateful, bitter, and spiteful. In fact, it's even more than that. I'm so angry that . . ."
3. Learn to recognize anger's roots: sadness or fear or a combination of the two. Sadness about broken dreams or promises, sadness about being betrayed or betraying one's self; fear of the future, of failure, of pain. Learn to recognize the roots of your own anger—in every situation.
4. Express it. Say it to the person with whom you're angry: "I am angry. I'm hurt, sad, and fearful, too." If you're angry with your child, express your feeling to your child. If it's your ex-spouse, express it to him or her.

This must be handled with discretion and wisdom. It's not helpful to make this into a spouse-bashing exercise escalating the emotional rift that already exists and forcing both sides to erect higher and thicker "walls."

In the transaction it is important that you express what you are feeling. Nothing more, nothing less. Don't make threats. Don't make accusations. Use "I feel" statements to express emotions. Even if the individual to whom you express your feelings refuses to listen, the encounter can be very cathartic. This can be done face to face or over the phone. You might practice your lines on a third party, asking for feedback.

If you can't say it, at least write it on paper and keep it on hand to read from time to time. This process can be helpful even if you don't send it to the person with whom you are angry.

5. Take small steps: decide on some small steps you can take to resolve the roots of your anger—usually fear or sadness. You don't have to be "out of control." You can determine to gain some control over the fear or

sadness driving your anger, so that the anger itself begins to subside.

6. Make the decision to forgive, maybe not today, but someday. This is a powerful step that will immeasurably help *you* heal. (You might not be able to accept this yet.)

7. Leave the past in the past. Set a date on which you will begin to leave the past in the past and build your future, but *without* anger. That is, don't bake the new cake— your new life—with anger as an ingredient. It's a lousy taste to stir into a recipe. Ruins the whole thing—and that "whole thing" is your new life.

8. Direct your anger appropriately. Direct your anger at the divorce, at the wreckage, and at the broken dreams—not at your ex-spouse, your children, or yourself.

9. Accept emotional polarization. It is possible to love someone and yet be so angry and hurt that you hate him or her also. Hate is not the opposite of love, indifference is. Perhaps you're so angry in part because you still love your ex-spouse? If so, it's normal. Painful, perhaps chaotic, but normal.

10. Take your anger to God. If you're angry with God, tell him. If you want to scream, scream—before God. (Right now you may not feel close to God. That's okay. He created you. He loves you, and he knows the depth of passion you feel. Take your stuff—all your stuff—to God.)

Venting anger, per se, is of some, but limited, value. It is more helpful to use the steps outlined above. If you're going to use your anger for anything, use it to propel yourself toward the goal of your own healing, your own growth, your own learning. Use it as a positive force to help you mature, mellow, and stabilize. Use your anger wisely, for your own growth and healing.

BARGAINING

This is another stage of attempting to deny the reality of divorce, this time by making trades, deals, or promises. It is still a stage of nonacceptance of the divorce. It is a last attempt to manipulate circumstances so as to avoid pain.

When facing the death of a loved one, it is not unusual to try to make deals with God. "If you let my loved one live, I'll become a missionary to Africa." "If you give us five more years together, I'll quit smoking and never drive over the speed limit."

Within divorce a spouse might similarly bargain with God. "If you help pull our marriage together, I'll do X, Y, and Z." Sometimes separated spouses will bargain with each other. "If you're willing to give it another try, I'll do X, Y, and Z." Sometimes deals are cut with in-laws or friends who seem able to exert leverage with the spouse.

The bargaining stage can get ugly if the person takes manipulative action to try to control the situation and head off the loss. Of course preventive action can be healthy and helpful, as when one partner says to the other, "I'm sorry. I've made some mistakes. I'll make some changes. Let's work at saving our marriage." But it is not healthy when it is aimed at *forcing* the divorce not to happen, allowing the bargaining "denier" (bargaining can be a second stage of denial) to continue living a fantasy.

For example, if a wife comes home and says she has filed for divorce, the husband may say, "No, if you stay, we'll get some counseling." That may be a healthy attempt at restoring a marriage. But it's not healthy if it's the fifth or sixth time the wife has filed for divorce, and the husband's plea for counseling is merely a manipulative ploy, a mechanism to avoid dealing with the painful reality of the divorce.

There may be less obvious ways and means of bargaining— as one attempts to win back one's lost self-esteem. At this stage a woman's dress might reveal more than while married. She might be more giddy and huggy than ever before. A man may begin wearing open shirts with gold chains, playing the role of the immature college sophomore. A formerly reserved person may frequent hot spots or engage in long and intimate conversations with just about anyone—or everyone.

These individuals are wrestling with damaged self-esteem, attempting to prove to themselves that they are still appealing, still of value. "Hey, world, I'm still pretty sharp. Do you see me?" Altering a self-identity seems a small price to pay to avoid pain: "If I dress or act differently, perhaps I won't hurt as badly. Perhaps someone new will notice and desire me." Or maybe the changes will draw one's spouse back. "You didn't know I could be like *this*, did you? Now what do you think of me? Could you love me again? Do you want the new me?"

Sometimes bargains work. Sometimes the spouse returns. More often, bargaining leads to the next stage of the grief cycle; the individual comes to the sad realization that the best attempts at cutting deals have accomplished nothing; the divorce is still going through, the self-esteem is still hopelessly low, and nothing is going to change. With the recognition of this reality, depression begins to weigh on the heart like an evil plague.

DEPRESSION

Depression is living in the valley of the shadow of death. Everything seems to stop. All is fear, sadness, and hurt. One realizes that the bullet couldn't be dodged. It has struck its mark and destroyed joy.

During this stage it is not unusual for a person to withdraw into a personal, emotional cocoon, temporarily suspending social relationships and activities. Some people cease caring about their appearance. Hope is lost. The future is black.

While it may be the most unbearable stage, it is also the first stage to real acceptance, to rebuilding a new life. It is a busy time internally as you start to understand that you are now alone. Single. The marriage is dead, gone. Facing those facts is the challenge of this stage, and facing them may require all the energy you have.

This is the time for friends to allow "space" for you to readjust. You need quietness not counsel. You need to weep, not talk too much.

If you're a friend, it's time to bring supper but not pressure anyone to eat it. It is the time for a phone call, "Thinking about you. Love you. Praying for you. Hang in there. This too shall pass." It is the winter of the grief cycle, the time when nights are long and cold. It is a time when the emotional circuitry is over-loaded. One feels spent without having lifted a finger. One can't concentrate on anything. Some people may not be able to sleep at all. Others may do nothing but sleep. One person may not eat anything for days. Another may eat constantly.

It is a time of feeling sadness and loneliness; a time of remembering what was and being profoundly saddened that it is gone and will never be again. It is a time of terror over the future, whether you left the marriage or were left.

It is such a painful stage that many people are willing to do almost anything to avoid it. Some hurl themselves into intimate relationships. Others become "manic," talking fast, working hard, keeping frantically busy, so as never to have a quiet moment, since those quiet moments lead toward despair. Some try to numb the pain with alcohol or drugs. Yes, this stage is "the valley of the shadow of death."

The longer one stays in this cocoon, alone and somewhat isolated, the more comfortable the cocoon can become. As difficult as it may be, it is important to work toward coming out of the cocoon. You might set a date on which you will, by choice, reenter the world. If your depression goes on for months and you can't begin the process of emerging, professional help is recommended.

ACCEPTANCE

This final stage in the grief cycle is the second stage of rebuilding. It is a turning point. In this stage the individual begins to think, perhaps hope, that there is a speck of light at the end of the tunnel. The depression becomes ever so slightly less agonizing.

You start to make the bed again or jog once a week. You might be surprised that you ate three meals in one day. You might feel like phoning a friend for lunch. You clean the house in case someone might drop over to visit. If life *is* going to go on, you just might want to join it.

SYMPTOMS OF ABNORMAL GRIEF

Keep in mind that normal grief is frequently experienced as heavy stress, and heavy stress normally brings about many seemingly abnormal reactions—abnormal as compared with the usual responses and feelings that one may have had prior to the onset of grief. Keep in mind that craziness during the grief cycle can be normal.

Abnormal grief frequently begins with an *underreaction*. While the individual experiencing abnormal grief is subject to the same emotional *factors* as the individual in normal grief, the *response* within abnormal grief (or unhealthy grief management) is muted, absent, or inappropriately calm; on the surface, there appear to be little or no feelings.

These extreme underreactions may be caused by many factors. Here are a few:

- childhood upbringing that taught one to deny feelings or pain;
- fear of losing control (fear of being overwhelmed by one's emotions and subsequent denial of the emotions' existence);
- a male's belief system that it's not "manly" for a man to grieve;
- a personality so badly crushed (perhaps during childhood, adolescence, or within a brutal marriage) that it is unable to experience normal feelings of sadness, fear, and grief;
- an anger level so profound that the individual fears he or she might overreact (e.g., commit murder) if feelings were allowed to exist;
- a need to show the other spouse that one is not hurting.

Unresolved grief issues are much like the remote control power boxes used to steer toy airplanes or cars. The individual's behavior, perception, and attitude are subconsciously controlled even though the individual may not see that he or she is being steered by the "remote" source.

Abnormal grief involves a high level of denial and repression of feelings (and frequently of facts as well). Because the individual *cannot* allow reality to exist, he or she creates some form of altered reality—which is just as real to this person as is the reality experienced by everyone else in the world. To give a silly analogy, the whole world may *not* see a ladder sticking up out of the ground. But the person in denial sees it, even climbs it, and from the top can see the world from a different perspective than anyone else—or so this person *thinks*.

In another analogy, the person in denial may not believe that there is a locomotive coming down the track. When everyone else screams and says he's in danger, he laughs at them. When the locomotive hits and plasters him against the wall on the side of the track, he responds, "The train wasn't there. I didn't get hit. I'm not hurt. Now just leave me alone."

Let's look at a few examples of how abnormal grief is precipitated by denial and repression. Consider the man who, very peacefully and in good emotional control, walked away from his marriage of twenty years. He claimed to have felt no pain, no sadness, some small anger, but no grief. He shortly became emotionally attached to another woman who had children the same age as his own. When this second relationship didn't work out, he found himself deeply depressed, desperately sad, weeping frequently, and grieving almost beyond his ability to bear.

He had simply avoided dealing with the pain of his marriage and divorce. He had numbed the pain of losing close and daily contact with his children, and he had used the new relationship to foster this avoidance. Not until the second relationship went up in flames did he experience a highly traumatic and deeply depressed reaction. In delaying his grief work, he later struggled in confusion and agony as he waded through a double dose of grief—from his marriage and from his second relationship.

Another example: A woman married seven years was deeply wounded when she found out that her husband had had a brief affair. They seemed to reconcile but she began to see her marriage as a tragic mistake. For the next several years she carried the memory, the sadness, and the anger associated with that betrayal. For religious reasons she swallowed her anger. She also denied her feelings of sadness and grief.

One morning she announced to her husband that she was going to get an attorney *that day* and as soon as possible get a divorce. She left the three children with him and moved to another city. Her grief had "gone underground," become too powerful to repress any longer, and driven her to precipitous actions that would not have been necessary, given a healthy grief experience.

Sometimes, the abnormal grief reaction draws the person to dealing with feelings and issues that bent and shaped him or her at a much younger stage of growth. This individual in the midst of divorce might go home and scream at mother and father for things that happened thirty years ago. This individual focuses energies on the past, avoiding the grief work at hand. The incorrect focus makes the person feel emotionally naked and vulnerable, precipitating a frightening sense of loss of control over emotions.

Sometimes these powerful feelings seem to come out of nowhere, indicating that they were *deeply* buried in the lower levels of consciousness. This experience can be somewhat like going for a walk on a slightly cloudy day and being hit by lightning.

The life of the individual experiencing an abnormal grief reaction can become incredibly altered. Old friendships may be abruptly terminated. Parents, siblings, or children may suddenly be rejected. One may suddenly make a major career change, move to another city, suddenly "see the light" and take up yoga and snake charming. The more irrational the behavior the more it is defended as being highly rational. Furious hostility erupting against specific people is frequently a symptom of abnormal grief reaction. Behavior detrimental to one's own existence may become commonplace. Substantial and long-term memory loss may be present.

An abnormal grief reaction may last a lifetime if one does not receive professional help.

Sadly, people experiencing an abnormal grief reaction usually live with so much denial and repression that they don't seek professional help until they have run into the same brick wall so many times that they are nearly hopeless.

As you consider your own situation, visualize the grief response on a continuum, from left to right, from crazy-but-normal, to calm-but-abnormal. Where do you stand? Because there may be some symptoms of abnormal grief within the normal grief experience, and vice versa, it is best to look at the overall picture of one's grief, to establish where it generally lies on the continuum.

SUCCESSFUL GRIEF WORK

No matter where you are in the grief process, as painful as it is, one of the best goals you can set for yourself is to gradually accept your part in and responsibility for the deterioration and dysfunction of the marriage (that is, for the puddle in which you find yourself). If you feel no responsibility for the death of the marriage, then you're a "victim," powerless to avoid similar future problems and pain. But if you were involved in the dysfunction and the deterioration of your marriage, then you have some control over your future, as you begin to rebuild. You can take steps to prevent this from happening again. An understanding of this is especially important for those who feel they were "victims" in the divorce, helplessly led before a judge only to watch a marriage die.

When you are alone and free from external pressures, try to relax, close your eyes, and say, "I am sad"; "I am angry"; or, "I am scared." Allow the feelings to ebb and flow. Let them wash over you like waves if they wish to do so. Feel them. Let them exist. They won't kill you.

You can develop a regular routine to help yourself through the grieving process. For example, you might consider setting aside a few minutes every day, perhaps fifteen to thirty minutes, to focus on your grief. Initially you may wish to take more than fifteen minutes. The point is to take *some* time every day, to focus specifically on your feelings. If you *regularly* allow yourself time to deal with those feelings, you *will* wade through them. (If you work at avoiding them, then rather than wading through the swamp of grief, you'll take the swamp with you.)

As you focus on your feelings, be careful not to spend too much time thinking about ways to manipulate the situation, get even with your ex-spouse, or win some power struggle. Those are means of hanging on to the past. We live with a hard reality: We have absolutely no control over the past. What has happened has happened, and, try as we might, we can't change it. Letting go is usually not pleasant, as you're letting go of precious dreams, hopes, goals, even a part of your self. Yet you cannot successfully enter the future if you are tied with chains to the past.

There is a time for holding on, hoping that the marriage may be reconciled. When that doesn't happen, you need to reach the "point of leaving," the time for admitting that your comprehensive attempts have been futile. There is a time to hope, and a time to let go and accept the finality of divorce. Allow yourself to say, "It is finished. It's truly over. I am alone again. Right now I feel . . ." and face your situation.

RECAP

Grief does not happen in the logical, sequential manner in which it is presented here. As a person moves through grief, it is completely normal for a person to bounce around from one stage to another, from stage two to four, then back to one, ahead to five, and then back to three.

No two people progress through the grief cycle at the same pace. Your ex-spouse may be dealing with depression when you are only at the stage of denial. Also, each stage is experienced uniquely by each individual. No two people experience the same stage the same way. Don't make the mistake of comparing your grief work with anyone else's.

One person will progress through the entire cycle within two months, while another person may be stuck in stage one for eight months. Having said that there is no "norm" for progressing through the grief cycle, let's now establish some approximate boundaries. While it may be possible to wade through the grief cycle in two to three weeks, that may be cutting it short. If the grieving goes on for more than a year, professional therapy would be appropriate. But know that counseling could be helpful at any stage of grief—even normal grief.

There are no short cuts to grief work. Healing takes time. But you can enhance and even speed up the process by regularly sharing feelings with people who care. Allowing another individual to care and perhaps bear some small part of the load can help immeasurably.

This diagram gives you an overview of the grief process.

The Grief Cycle

New Wholeness

Shock—This can't be happening to me!

Denial—I won't let this happen!
—I never lose, and I won't this time.
—I'll fight you in the courts.
—You can't make it without my money.

Anger—Let me tell you about the jerk I used to live with.
—I'll show you! I'll make it better without you!
—The kids think you're a creep.
—Maybe a letter bomb would work.

Bargaining—Perhaps if I try a new hair style . . .
—What if I changed to meet his or her need?
—What if I became a lion tamer or a nightclub singer?
—What if we moved to a new city?

Depression—My life is ruined.
—There is no hope.
—Everything is dark around me.
—I'm so sad and afraid.
—I'm too old to start again.
—I'll be alone forever.
—The children are gone too.
—Why keep trying?
—Life hurts.
—Who cares anyway?
—Perhaps it would hurt less if I killed myself.

Rebuilding—I believe in . . .
Rebuilding—My next relationships will . . .
Rebuilding—I can make it!
Rebuilding—I'm going to be all right.
Rebuilding—Next year's vacation . . .
Rebuilding—I need some new friends.
Rebuilding—I think I'll read a book.
Rebuilding—Maybe I'll go back to school.
Rebuilding—Tomorrow I start jogging again.
Rebuilding—Perhaps I'll call Chris.
Rebuilding—I need a haircut.
Rebuilding—I should clean this apartment.
Rebuilding—I will probably have to get an apartment.
Acceptance—There is nothing I can do to avoid the inevitable.
Now what am I going to do to survive?

QUESTIONS FOR REFLECTION

1. At what stage in the grief cycle would you place yourself now? What feelings are you having? How do those feelings help you identify where you are in the grieving process? Write a paragraph or more describing your journey to date in the grief cycle.
2. Draw a continuum of grief, the left being crazy-but-normal and the right being calm-but-abnormal. What symptoms in your life tell you where you are on the continuum?
3. What is a reasonable amount of time for withdrawal from the rest of the world as one goes through grief? Name some tasks and goals that might be helpful during this time of withdrawal.
4. How can close, same-sex friends be supportive as one wades through the grief work of divorce? How well supported are you in your grief work? What can you do to find more support?
5. What healing tasks lay ahead of you as you complete your own journey through the grief cycle?

ACTION ITEMS

1. Make a small collage representing your ex-spouse. Use old mementos, pictures, or whatever may be appropriate. Focus on the representation for a few minutes each day. Express your feelings verbally: "I am angry. I hate you. I still love you. I am deeply sad, hurt, and bitter." When you're done, get up and leave the collage. Move your attention and energy to something else for the remainder of the day. This allows you to work through some of your feelings toward your ex-spouse, leaving you more free from those feelings the rest of the day.
2. Begin writing a letter to your ex-spouse. Put on paper everything you wish you could say. Fully express your feelings. Don't try to be rational. Rather, try to be thorough. Express everything you feel or have felt. Take as many days, weeks, or months as you may wish, but

be thorough. *Don't mail it!* This letter is for your own healing, not for punishing or manipulating your ex-spouse. After writing it, put it away for a while. Add to it as you need to express your feelings. Someday, when you have fully said everything you wanted to say, have a small ceremony and burn it.

3. If you are especially struggling with crazy emotional swings, purchase and read the book *The Crazy Time* by Abigail Trafford. We highly recommend it.

FOR SPIRITUAL GROWTH

1. Read Philippians 4:6–7. Then openly tell God everything you are feeling. Don't hold back anything. Share your sadness, your anger, your fear and pain, your grief—all of it—with the only One who is truly strong enough to help you bear it.

2. Read James 1:1–20. Ask God for the wisdom necessary to properly handle some of the overwhelming tasks facing you right now. One of these tasks may be dealing with your grief.

3. Read Psalm 73. Identify some of the stages the psalmist seems to be facing: anger, bargaining, depression. Write a psalm of your own.

‡

CHAPTER 2

FEELINGS: OH, WOE, WHOA, FEELINGS!

I am benumbed and badly crushed.

Psalm 38:8 (NASB)

For a while I thought I was going to go crazy. Sometimes I'd cry for hours. Then I'd get scared, I mean really terrified. Once I found myself fantasizing about killing myself and my mate. That was when I began to think I was really losing it.

For many people, going through divorce is like walking through a tumultuous, turbulent hurricane that destroys one's whole framework of life. Hurricanes frequently spawn tornados, and divorce can spawn wild emotional swings.

Nobody walks through the fire of divorce without being burned. Both spouses are wounded. Children are confused and torn at least as much as their divorcing parents. Parents of divorcing people are wounded, as are their friends.

Those spouses and children who most *seem* to escape the pain of divorce are frequently the most wounded. Their wounds are often most profound and the fact that they feel little pain only demonstrates the magnitude of the wound. To feel no pain when going through divorce often indicates that the pain is too awful to allow into conscious thought.

AM I CRAZY OR WHAT?

At some point in the separation-divorce process, many people experience staggering and frightening emotional swings that almost eliminate their ability to function. Fear—so real it can be tasted. Sadness—so deep they wonder if they will ever again feel good about anything. Anger—so powerful that some talk of murder, suicide, or both. These emotions come and go like huge waves threatening to overwhelm or perhaps destroy the individual.

This crazy time, which may go on for weeks or months, makes real sense if you understand that a bond is being broken. Imagine two smooth pine boards glued together and pressed in a vise for twenty-four hours. To drive them apart, even using a sharp chisel, you will rip and tear the boards, with parts of each remaining forever attached to the other. Similarly, in marriage two people have been melded to each other, possibly for years. They have shared the most intimate aspects of life. Their identities have become intertwined. They are bonded—glued together. The ripping and tearing that occurs in the dissolution of a marriage is massively painful. People exhibit many of the symptoms of a human organism under deep stress.

Know that when going through divorce there is no such thing as normal. It can be normal for feelings to be running amuck, and it can be normal to feel crazy. Just as it's normal to react to the pain of slamming one's finger in a door, it's also normal to react to the pain at the end of a marriage. But given the wide variety in human nature, no two people necessarily react in the same way.

Divorcing people frequently report being surprised at the depth and strength of their own emotions. They find themselves laughing "too" loudly, crying "too" frequently or hard, being "too" frightened by small things.

Imagine a pot filled with cold water and then placed on a red-hot stove. The water will take five or more minutes to heat up, finally reaching the boiling point. But imagine a pot sitting on the stove, being kept at 210 degrees Fahrenheit (just two degrees below the boiling point). Just a little more heat and the water instantly boils over.

So it is with divorce, emotions, and stress: Little things can quickly make the pot boil over. A year ago a discourteous store clerk was no big deal. You could walk away from the supermarket feeling just fine about yourself and perhaps a little sorry for the poor stressed-out clerk. Now the rude clerk can almost ruin an entire day!

Relax. Craziness is normal—considering the stress you're under.

PAIN HAS A PURPOSE

The emotional pain of divorce is real, so real that some people try to ignore it or deny its existence. Imagine that a person has received a physical wound—a deep gash or a fractured bone. Imagine what could happen if the person decided to ignore the pain and go about life as if nothing were wrong. The deep cut could become infected. The broken bone might cut off the supply of blood to vital organs, causing death. If the break were not fatal, it most likely would heal in a crooked manner, permanently impairing the individual's movement. In short, ignoring wounds usually causes further problems.

Emotions must not be ignored. Rather, they must be understood and dealt with. To ignore them, to deny the pain, is usually to prolong the infection. As in dealing with physical wounds, postponing treatment only makes problems more difficult (probably even more painful) to diagnose and correct.

Has anyone ever told you, "Don't cry. Don't be scared. Don't be angry"? People who use such phrases think they are helping to lead us away from a feeling. For example, a four-year-old child is separated from Mother in a dense crowd at an airport. As the child cries, a kind person stops, picks up the child, determines the problem, and says, "Don't cry. Don't be afraid. We'll find your mommy."

While the child may be able to summon enough strength to shut off the tears, the fear will remain until Mother is found again. So it is with any feeling. We may be able to *act* as if we're okay, but unresolved feelings remain until they're resolved. When someone says, "Don't be afraid," or, "Don't be angry," that person is asking you to do something unhealthy and frequently impossible: to not feel what you feel.

Feelings are healthy, powerful, natural, and God-given gifts—to be used to direct us. Feelings are messengers; they tell us things. When we listen to them, we are able to react intelligently.

WHAT ARE FEELINGS?

When the human personality is placed under a severe stress load, as for example when one goes through divorce, three items—fact, thinking, and feeling—frequently become confusingly enmeshed with one another. But as you learn to separate each form of "head work" from the others, you gain self-knowledge and the ability to walk toward wholeness.

Facts are always facts. If a coat is red, it's red. If the sun is shining, it's shining. Facts don't change.

Thinking interprets facts. What one *thinks* about facts is an *interpretation*, usually highly personalized in nature, of the facts. One may not *like* red coats. One person may think that sunshine is good, and another may think it harmful. The thinking process is always interpretive. It's based upon past experience, how one sees the facts, and how able one is to form reasonable hypotheses regarding those experiences and perceptions. Thinking focuses opinion.

Feeling is an internal reaction to and general sense of these facts, opinions, perceptions, and experiences. Feeling is a subjective experience, unique to the individual. Feelings are not right or wrong, good or bad. There are no ways one "should" or "should not" feel. Feelings just are. They may not be the same as anyone else's, but they are right for us, considering who we are and the circumstances we're in.

For example, if you have a toothache, and I don't, it's not up to me to tell you that your toothache doesn't make any sense. It's *your* ache, your feeling, not mine. Your ache makes clear sense to you. It hurts!

Some people waste energy trying to compare what they feel with what others feel. Going through divorce, a husband may be intensely angry. The wife may be sad or afraid. The fact that neither is experiencing the other's feeling is irrelevant. Each person's own history and situation cause specific and unique feelings.

CAN FEELINGS BE TRUSTED?

Can one's feelings be trusted? The answer is a qualified yes. They can be trusted to tell you that you are hurting or under strong emotional stress. They need to be heard. They *are* telling you *something*. Just *what* they are trying to tell you may be confusing at first, but as you give yourself time to actively listen to them, they can lead you to understanding. As you decode their messages, you can identify steps you can take to address them.

Feelings can, and frequently do, mask themselves. Gender-based programming can be one factor, as sadness and fear in males is frequently misdiagnosed as anger; anger in females is frequently misdiagnosed as sadness or fear.

Our culture teaches men and women to *express* feelings differently. Men are usually taught that it's all right to express aggression and anger; not so with sadness or fear. Years ago when I was a skinny sophomore in high school, I played football. I'll never forget being "double teamed" by two semihumanoid gorillas, weighing 235 pounds each. At 160 pounds, I had to get past those two apes and then tackle the ball carrier. Their task was to stop me by whatever means they felt appropriate and necessary.

It hurt. Bashing into them really hurt. They would knock me flat on my back. I saw stars almost every time I tried it. I wanted to scream in pain. I wanted to go crawl into some dark space and ache and perhaps even cry. But my coach was always there saying, "Okay, next time you run into them, do it harder. Show them who's in charge out here. Knock them on their butts!"

The message was clear: Don't feel pain. Don't feel scared. Don't feel sad. Take all those feelings and transform them into the most powerful expression of aggression and anger that you can muster. That's what many men are taught as boys. Little boys aren't supposed to cry when hurt or scared. They're supposed to get tough, be aggressive.

Women, on the other hand, are taught not to express anger or aggression. It's all right for them to be sad or scared, but get too mad about something and they're likely to be rejected or punished. She's given permission to cry and withdraw in helplessness, but let a little girl whop her friend on the head with a doll or punch her on the nose, and Mother is there telling her that nice girls don't do that sort of thing. (And, as teenagers, most girls aren't playing tackle football.)

What we have, then, is a lot of men who have been taught to turn most feelings into anger and/or aggression, and a lot of women who have been taught to turn most feelings into sadness or fear. That can get pretty confusing, especially when both parties are hurting over the same issue—let's say divorce—but seem to be expressing two completely different feelings.

Not all misdiagnoses are gender-based, and our thoughts and opinions can confuse us as we identify feelings.

Here's an example. Sally, recently divorced, is terrified— at being alone with the kids, trying to be both mom and dad, being responsible for the home maintenance and all the bills, and having no job. (It's a legitimate fear. It's normal and natural that she should feel this way.)

Sally is a religious person, brought up in a very religious home. She believes it's wrong (even sinful) to feel afraid, since "God is in control of every circumstance." (She doesn't *feel* that God's very much in control of her particular circumstance, but to admit that feeling would border on heresy in her understanding of things.)

So Sally doesn't "feel" fear. To do so would be to challenge both her parents' teaching and her own faith. Rather than feeling her fear, Sally puts into its place some other feeling or directive, maybe sadness, since her parents always let her express sadness. It might even be joy; she may believe that since God is in control, the divorce is somehow going to end up being a wonderfully positive experience.

When the fear persists, Sally may attempt another approach. She may, for example, attempt to overcome it by becoming highly active in her church. She may suddenly decide to go on for a graduate degree in psychology. She may attempt to evade its constant presence by just becoming active, period, all the time, with no rest stops. (Do you recognize signs of unhealthy coping mechanisms?)

The greater the trauma of one's childhood years, the more pain carried during adolescence or adulthood, the more likely it is for that person to have a hard time identifying and getting in touch with real feelings. But facing and identifying feelings is critical to an individual's healing.

Let's look at a failure to do this. Consider the male who suppresses his sadness regarding divorce; he's lost daily contact with his children, and this hurts him badly. But he doesn't let himself "feel" the sadness. Perhaps he doesn't even know how to feel sadness, and so he becomes increasingly angry with his ex-wife. Soon he finds himself being constantly frustrated (a form of anger) with just about everything in the world, almost as if the world were responsible for his predicament.

Or consider the woman who ignores her anger over the divorce and yet finds herself crying (thus expressing sadness) much of the time. She can't figure out why she's in tears so often, since she doesn't "think" she's all that sad about things.

Both are misdiagnosing (missing) their real feelings, one through suppression of the real feeling, and the other by a thinking process. It's not hard to misdiagnose feelings. They can be elusive, especially if one is in emotional turmoil.

FEELINGS MANAGEMENT

A person is far more in control when able to *verbalize* the actual feelings being experienced. Since feelings are usually the "driver" pushing the gas pedal, giving energy to actions, as you separate feelings from thought, you can better control your actions and attitudes.

Many people fear that if they allow the depth of their feelings to emerge, they'll either be controlled by those feelings or lose control over them. *What if my feelings get out of control and I can't handle them?*

Fear of sadness itself is sometimes terrifying. *What if I start crying and can never stop? What if I become hysterical?* The fact is that if you let go and have a good cry, you will eventually "cry yourself out," and the wave of sadness will again wash out to sea.

You've probably heard someone say, "I was so mad I couldn't think," or, "I was so mad I couldn't talk." Actually, neither of these statements is accurate. Humans can feel and think at the same time. And conscious feelings don't control our actions unless we decide to let them do so. No matter how deeply one may feel about something, one still will consciously decide what to do about that feeling. Feelings generally do not control a person unless the individual allows them to do so and decides to use being out of control as an excuse to act out.

Interestingly, the more energy one gives to suppressing feelings, the more they tend to demand attention in some form or another. The more energy one gives to holding them down, the more energy they require to be held down. They don't just fade away. It is far more productive to use one's energy to manage them—and then get actively involved in problem solving.

As you listen to your feelings, you can learn many things, including where they come from, why they remain, with what other feelings they may be associated, how to gain control in your life so the roller coaster ride begins to subside, how to care for yourself, and how to communicate effectively with others.

Recognize Your Feelings

To learn how to use feelings to grow toward wholeness, one must begin by stating, as clearly as possible, just what one is feeling. Is it anger? Hurt? Hesitancy? Fear? Terror? Sadness? Hopelessness? Be specific. Name it!

Diagnosis is half the battle. For example, if one flips a wall switch and the light bulb doesn't go on, something's wrong. It could be in the switch. It could be a burned out bulb. The power might be off. Before replacing the switch or the bulb, or before calling the power company with a complaint, it's wise to diagnose why the bulb isn't lighting up.

So it is with feelings. Basic question: What emotion are you feeling? Listen to your heart. Don't be afraid to name it. (What's the worst that can happen if you name your feeling?) Name five or six similar emotions. For example, *fear*: timid or shy; terror; embarrassed; hopeless about the future; hesitant; reserved; inhibited. These are different facets of fear.

If you're not good at recognizing your feelings, refer to the list provided at the end of this chapter. Pick feelings from the list. Start learning to monitor your feelings *all* the time. If you can't recognize what you're feeling, then those unrecognized feelings will control your behavior and you won't even know it. You'll be the victim of your feelings.

Internally Admit the Depth of the Feeling

A person may recognize an emotion but not *internally admit* the degree to which it is present. It's often frightening. Our upbringing and assumptions about how life is supposed to work frequently superimpose a framework of "shoulds" upon us at this point. That framework, whether it's religious, one we brought with us from our childhood, or from any other source, often gets in the way of our feeling what's really there, by telling us that we are supposed to feel something other than what we're feeling.

Consider Sally, whose parents or religious beliefs never let her express or feel her fear. Now she's getting divorced and is terribly frightened, but she still doesn't have "permission" to feel it. Her parents' "shoulds" are superimposed on her fear.

As you admit the depth of your feeling, you may be forced to reevaluate what you believe. *If what I was taught doesn't work, what do I believe now?!*

In the next chapter, on grief, we will delve deeper into God's word on emotions, especially anger. But here let me just say that God knows you better than you know yourself. As 1 Samuel 16:7 says, God sees the heart. Why try to hide the force of your feelings from Someone who already knows? What is there to gain by not being completely open with him—and yourself? Why not admit internally, *I'm feeling very frightened right now*. Or, *I'm so sad I can feel it in my chest*.

Express Your Feeling Verbally to Yourself

Now that you've admitted it internally, give yourself permission to name your feelings out loud, with no attempt at "padding" it or making it less than it is. "I'm hurt and scared." "I don't know which way to turn. I feel lost." "I'm so angry I find myself fantasizing about killing my ex." "I am terrified about what may happen to the kids now that my spouse and I have divorced." Express it. Say it out loud to yourself.

Express It to Someone Else

Share your feelings with another person. It is wiser and safer to share your feelings with someone of *your own sex*. (Men will usually find this more difficult than women, and those emotionally damaged during childhood will often find it difficult.)

The danger of sharing with a member of the opposite sex right now is that you are vulnerable to being infatuated with them. Someone may be a good listener but that says absolutely nothing about your mutual ability to make a *healthy* connection. Actually, the less vulnerable you feel as you go through divorce, the more vulnerable you're likely to be.

Also, don't confuse "dumping" your hurt, anger, and fear with the issue of trust. Dumping and trusting are not the same thing. People may listen to you, but that doesn't mean that you (a) should trust them or (b) are ready to risk trusting again. You might not know for a very long time whether you have the basis for a good relationship with *anybody*.

Seek out same-sex friends who will be willing to offer support and nurturing. Divorce-recovery support groups are an excellent resource, since everyone in the group is facing much the same experience.

Keep your emotional vulnerability in mind at all times. Wisdom and discretion are your best friends.

FEELINGS AND YOUR CHILDREN

If you're a parent, you may worry that you don't know what to do about your children's feelings when you haven't yet figured out what to do about your own feelings. You can help your children as you teach them to (a) recognize, (b) admit, (c) express, and (d) direct their feelings. You may have to be very sensitive to them and listen more than talk, as they may direct very difficult feelings toward you. Keep reminding yourself, you're doing this for their healing.

Above all, keep recalling that as you go through divorce, your children, no matter their age, are likely experiencing the same kinds of feelings you are having. Work hard on your own healing. Work hard at allowing them to express their feelings. The better you are able to heal yourself, the more you'll find your children will be healed, too.

FAKING HAPPINESS

As you go through divorce, you can fake it as much as you like to convince your friends that you're doing well and that your life is just peachy. But you don't *have* to pretend to be happy when you're dying on the inside. You know how it is. You're walking through the grocery store or coming out of church and someone says, "Hey, how's it going?" and you respond with a big smile, "Oh, fine, thanks." The words are happy, but in the mirror your eyes tell you that you're sad.

If you want to tell them that you're not doing very well right now, that you cry a lot, and that today you're doing fair but that doesn't mean that yesterday wasn't terrible and tomorrow's a little scary, go ahead.

Those who seem most to need you to project a happy face are themselves the ones who have the greatest problems with their own feelings. Don't "play to them." They're not a very good audience. In the end, they'll only try to make you as separated from your real feelings as they are from their own.

Projecting a constant "I'm happy" when you're suffering on the inside may help you fool a few people in the crowd, but it drains energy and after a while you begin to ask, "Why bother? Why pretend?"

Actually, that's a good question that may lead to a first step in finding some internal peace. In ancient Greece the written inscription over the Oracle at Delphi read, "Know thyself." Much of this "knowing" is the knowledge of what one *feels*.

The alternatives are simple: Learn to identify and address your feelings or they'll control you. The more you ignore or deny them, the more they'll control you. Rather than fight them, learn to seek the way of internal peace. Seek to be at peace with God, with yourself, with your world, and even with your ex.

The more you practice this the more you'll find that your internal compass stabilizes. You do have a compass. It's a spiritual compass and was built into you by God. Seek it. Seek him. Seek internal peace. Then let the feelings occur as they will.

EMOTIONS AS MOTIVATORS

Feelings can be tremendous motivators. Rather than allowing the normal fear (sometimes expressed as terror) of divorce frighten you into inaction, why not use it to your advantage, energize new plans for yourself. Hunters charged by angry bears have been known to be crippled or motivated by fear. Some have frozen, unable to move; others shot all their bullets and then leapt to tall branches of trees. Both are "fear responses." What's yours? How can you begin to use your fear to enable you to take control of your situation? If you say, "I can't," then you won't. If you say, "Okay, maybe I can," you'll at least explore your alternatives. Who knows what you'll discover?

If you're angry, rather than sitting around scheming revenge or loathing yourself, why not use the anger as a motivator to accomplish some good things for yourself? Anger may be the most powerful and most usefully harnessed emotion of all, as one quietly but resolutely decides, *I'm not going to live like this any longer. Something's going to change.*

Even sadness can be used to set a life toward wholeness and healing. "I don't want to be sad like this for much longer now" can provide real direction, helping you out of circumstances and perceived entrapments that seem desperate. Ask yourself, *What small things can I do to move me away from this sadness? Am I really ready to leave it behind?*

On paper all of this may look simple, but it's not. On the other hand, it is possible—and helpful!

WILL I EVER FEEL HAPPY AGAIN?

The feeling of joy is often conspicuously absent in the early stages of divorce recovery. Happy or joyful feelings may be fleetingly present ("Phew, no more dealing with that jerk!"), but the predominant feelings most divorcing people experience are derivatives of sadness, fear, and anger. Often people ask, "Will I always feel lousy?" The answer is simple: No. The time will come when you begin to feel normal and happy again.

Meanwhile, as you struggle through divorce, follow these bits of counsel.

First, don't miss the tiny joys that are all around you. Birds still sing every day. There is still the small child who lisps, "I did it all by myself, Mom!" while the buttons are all wrong on the coat, the hat is pulled on askew, and the shoes are on the wrong feet. Stop and note the beauty of the first snowfall; the first buds of spring; the crunch of leaves underfoot in the fall; the wonder of an unclouded starry night; the smell of logs burning in the fireplace; the loveliness of a flaming pink and orange sunset. You still can enjoy the wind on your face; the sunshine warming your back; the scent of a flower; a squirrel frisking up a tree and chattering at an overweight and panting hound. Sometimes we have to look for the little joys, but they are always there. Look for them—especially if you're convinced they won't make any difference anyway. (They will!)

The second tip is this: Don't miss the wisdom and maturing that can come to you through suffering. It has been said that human beings don't really grow or change until the pain of not changing exceeds the pain of changing. This is very difficult but accurate wisdom. Use this painful moment in your life to absorb the very best insight, maturity, growth, and wisdom that you can. Don't waste your suffering. Learn. Grow.

As you wade through the swamp of divorce, keep on reminding yourself: Take one day at a time. One day may be horrible, the next mildly better, and the next wretched. Somewhere between perfectly awful days you'll probably find a day or two that seem fairly nice. Enjoy the good ones when you have them. Don't begin "forecasting" your doomed future. The feelings will eventually begin to normalize, and you will one day be happy again.

Your feelings—many different feelings—are like the ocean tide. One feeling will predominate for a while and then wash out, only to return later. Let it happen. Relax. Take one day at a time, for as many days as it takes to get to the far side of the swamp.

FEELING WORDS

Abandoned	Attractive	Careless	Cut
Accepted	Aware	Caring	Damned
Accused	Awestruck	Carried away	Daring
Aching	Badgered	Cautious	Deceived
Adventurous	Baited	Certain	Deceptive
Affectionate	Battered	Chased	Degraded
Aggravated	Beaten	Cheated	Delighted
Aggressive	Beautiful	Cheerful	Demeaned
Agony	Belittled	Choked (up)	Demoralized
Agreeable	Belligerent	Close	Dependent
Alienated	Bereaved	Cold	Depressed
Alive	Betrayed	Comfortable	Deprived
Alone	Bitter	Comforted	Deserted
Aloof	Bored	Competitive	Desirable
Alluring	Bothered	Complacent	Desirous
Amazed	Bound-up	Complete	Despair
Amused	Boxed-in	Confident	Desperate
Angry	Brave	Conflicted	Destroyed
Anguished	Breathless	Confused	Different
Annoyed	Bristling	Considerate	Dirty
Anxious	Broken-up	Consumed	Disappointed
Apart	Bruised	Content	Disconnected
Apologetic	Bubbly	Cool	Disgraced
Appreciative	Bugged	Coy	Disgruntled
Apprehensive	Burdened	Crabby	Disgusted
Approved	Burned	Cranky	Distant
Argumentative	Burned-up	Crappy	Distraught
Aroused	Callous	Crazy	Distressed
Astonished	Calm	Critical	Distrusted
Assertive	Capable	Criticized	Distrustful
Attached	Captivated	Crushed	Dominated
Attacked	Carefree	Cuddly	Domineering
Attentive	Careful	Curious	Doomed

Double-crossed
Down
Dreadful
Eager
Ecstatic
Edgy
Elated
Embarrassed
Empty
Enraged
Enraptured
Enthusiastic
Enticed
Esteemed
Exasperated
Exhilarated
Exposed
Fascinated
Flattered
Foolish
Forced
Forceful
Fortunate
Forward
Friendly
Frightened
Frustrated
Full
Funny
Furious
Generous
Genuine
Giddy
Giving
Grateful
Greedy
Grim
Grouchy
Grumpy
Guarded
Happy-go-
    lucky
Hard
Hassled

Hateful
Healthy
Helpful
Helpless
Hesitant
High
Hollow
Hopeful
Horrified
Hostile
Humiliated
Hung Up
Hurt
Hyper
Ignorant
Impatient
Important
Impotent
Impressed
Incompetent
Incomplete
Independent
Innocent
Insecure
Insignificant
Insincere
Inspired
Insulted
Intimate
Intolerant
Involved
Irate
Irked
Irresponsible
Irritated
Jealous
Jittery
Joyous
Left out
Lively
Lonely
Loose
Lost
Loving

Low
Lucky
Lustful
Mad
Malicious
Mean
Miserable
Misunderstood
Moody
Mystified
Nasty
Nervous
Numb
Obsessed
Offended
Open
Ornery
Out of control
Overwhelmed
Overjoyed
Pampered
Panicky
Paralyzed
Patient
Peaceful
Peeved
Perceptive
Perturbed
Petrified
Phony
Pleased
Powerless
Pressured
Proud
Pulled apart
Put-down
Puzzled
Quarrelsome
Quiet
Raped
Ravished
Ravishing
Real
Refreshed

Regretful
Rejected
Rejecting
Relaxed
Relieved
Removed
Repulsed
Repulsive
Resentful
Resistant
Responsible
Responsive
Revengeful
Rotten
Ruined
Safe
Satiated
Satisfied
Scared
Scolded
Scorned
Screwed
Secure
Seduced
Seductive
Self-centered
Self-conscious
Selfish
Separated
Shattered
Shocked
Shot-down
Shy
Sickened
Silly
Sincere
Sinking
Smart
Smothered
Smug
Sneaky
Snowed
Soft
Soothed

Sorry	Sympathetic	Trustful	Violated
Spiteful	Tainted	Ugly	Violent
Spontaneous	Tender	Unapproachable	Voluptuous
Squelched	Tense	Unaware	Vulnerable
Starved	Terrific	Uncertain	Warm
Stiff	Terrified	Uncomfortable	Weak
Stifled	Thrilled	Under control	Whipped
Stimulated	Ticked	Understanding	Whole
Strangled	Tickled	Understood	Wild
Strong	Tight	Unfriendly	Willing
Stubborn	Timid	Unhappy	Wiped-out
Stunned	Tired	Unimportant	Withdrawn
Stupid	Tolerant	Unimpressed	Wishful
Subdued	Tormented	Unstable	Wonderful
Submissive	Torn	Upset	Worried
Successful	Tortured	Uptight	Worthy
Suffocated	Trapped	Useful	Wounded
Sure	Tremendous	Valuable	Zapped
Sweet	Tricked	Valued	

QUESTIONS FOR REFLECTION

1. In your childhood, what feelings were you not allowed to experience or express? How does what you learned in that family situation affect you now?

2. Name several feelings you've had within the past week. Give them specific names: anger, sadness, fear, depression, joy. . . .

3. When you don't want to feel a particular emotion, what techniques do you use to avoid it? What impact has this had on your relationships? Could this have been a factor in your divorce? How?

4. What one feeling is most difficult for you to handle? Why?

5. What is the strongest feeling you deal with repeatedly? What circumstances seem to elicit that feeling?

6. What thoughts come to mind as you consider turning strong and debilitating feelings into motivators for your own healing? Is this transition even possible? If so, how

might you turn the feeling you listed in question 4, above, into a positive, energizing force?

ACTION ITEMS

1. For at least one month keep a daily written list of your feelings (purpose: self-monitoring; learning to recognize feelings and see what circumstances set them off; using this information to turn that feeling into a positive motivator).
2. Ask several people who know you well what feelings or emotions they see you repressing or hiding. Note what each says and look for patterns (purpose: self-discovery; finding areas in which you may be repressing or suppressing feelings or memories).
3. List feelings that you were not permitted to experience or express as a child. See if you can make correlations between that family situation and your present family situation. Write any insights down on paper (purpose: tracking the correlation between what you learned as a child and how you acted out that lesson in an adult family system).
4. Write down at least one strong feeling with which you struggle. Write down at least three positive actions you might take to begin turning that feeling into a positive motivation toward your own healing and growth.

FOR SPIRITUAL GROWTH

1. Read the first chapter of the biblical book of Job. What emotions do you think Job was experiencing? Do you think God understood Job's emotions, or do you think God was playing with Job's life? How do you relate to Job's response in verse 21?
2. Read Psalm 23. What might David have been experiencing when he wrote verse 4? What does "the valley of the shadow of death" mean to you at this time in your life?

3. Read Psalm 121, substituting the words *me* and *my* for *you* and *your*. Copy this short psalm onto a note card and post in a visible place. Read it daily.
4. Read Luke 22:41–45. What emotions was Jesus probably experiencing? Write them down. Do you think God ("Father") understood Jesus' emotional suffering? Do you think God understands yours?

‡

CHAPTER 3

STRESSED OUT!

I had a knot in my stomach for weeks. I knew I was on overload, but didn't know how to get off of it. There were so many major decisions to make, and my feelings were like riding a roller coaster. I felt like a frayed knot.

Years ago, playing a pick-up game of football, one of my friends got knocked on the head. None of us saw it happen, but we saw the results: This stable, quiet, fun-loving guy started acting strange.

He asked the same questions over and over. "What happened to me? How did I get here? Where's my car?" After we all took turns answering his questions five or six times each, it dawned on us that Dave wasn't fooling around. He'd had his "bell rung." He'd been knocked coo-coo. He was trying to reorient himself to the world. One of the guys took him home. After answering the same questions another ten or fifteen times, Dave's wife decided to take him to the hospital, where he stayed overnight for observation. The next day he was released, and has been fine ever since.

Divorce is often like that. People hurt so badly and feel so disoriented that they ask the same questions over and over:

Why did it happen? How could he/she do this to me?

How could God let this happen? Where is God when I need him?

How can I make my ex hurt as badly as I hurt?

Did I deserve what I got?

What future could I possibly have now?

Will I hurt this badly forever?

Why does it hurt so badly?

Does everyone going through divorce feel like this?

Why am I so angry if I really don't care anymore?

I feel confused: How can hurt, hate, and love be so closely related?

I thought I knew him/her. How could I have been so wrong? How could I have picked him/her to marry?

Picture a cartoon of a person in stress: hair sticking straight out; bags under the eyes; shock waves around the head, as if the skull were a bell being gonged by a clapper-brain. There's that perplexed, intense look: Where am I and how did I get here?

But if you're going through divorce, it's no longer a cartoon. The stress is yours and it is real. Divorce can be one of the most traumatic events you will ever face.

When the human personality or soul is stressed, the body responds, preparing itself to either fight the "enemy" or flee to safety. The heart beats faster. Adrenaline shoots into the bloodstream. Breathing rates increase. You may have felt it while driving the freeway. Some jerk swerves into your lane, forcing you to flee—slam on the brakes and/or head for the ditch. For a moment you can feel your heart pound, your muscles tense. For several minutes after the event you feel unnerved, wiped out.

Consider a second scenario: You're David facing Goliath the giant. You could run away, but you choose to face the enemy and fight. Again, your body shifts into overdrive. In self-protection you give it all you've got. In a few minutes the battle is over. You go back to your tent and collapse until your bodily functions return to normal.

Now think about your own situation: days, months, maybe years of constant, heavy emotional stress. The individual lives in a state of heightened anxiety, higher blood pressure, more adrenaline in the bloodstream, higher heart rate. Is it any wonder, then, that other symptoms frequently accompany stress, such as the tendency to overeat or undereat; a desire to sleep most of the time or not at all; bowel problems, including colitis; stomach problems, including ulceration; migraine headaches; stiffness in the neck or back; greater susceptibility to colds, flu, and other illnesses; heart-related illnesses.

Living with a constant state of heightened anxiety and stress frequently causes real physical problems that are brought on because of one's emotional state. The body frequently gives little hints that something's wrong with the soul. All of this is normal—lousy, but normal.

Although I have no actual clinical studies to back it up, my own informal survey of practicing physicians indicates that 50 to 75 percent of the illnesses they treat are psychosomatic in origin—brought about as a result of a sick soul, a wounded or struggling personality.

The mind exerts tremendous and powerful influence over the body. If you doubt it, read Victor Frankl's *Man's Search for Meaning*, in which he recounts the stories of people in Nazi death camps; losing the desire to live, many simply laid down and died. Divorce frequently makes people feel as if they would like to roll over and never wake up.

LIFESTYLE PROFILE

The following Lifestyle Profile can help you take an inventory of your current stress level. Here's how the profile works:

Step one: Read through the profile and, as indicated, give yourself a score on each item. For example, for the first item, eating out, give yourself three points if you eat out two to four times per week. If you eat out eight to ten times per week, give yourself six points. More than ten times per week gives you ten points. Pick one answer that most closely describes your lifestyle. For some items, such as chemical stressors, you should give yourself points for any applicable personal habits.

Step two: Add up your subtotal points for each major section—Eating Habits, Alcohol and Drugs, Physical Activity, and so forth. One note of caution: In the Recent Life Changes category, your subtotal will be 5, 10, 15, or 30, not the total number of points you have for questions 1 through 43.

Step three: Go to the end of the inventory and list the subtotals for all major sections. Find your total score.

LIFESTYLE PROFILE[1]

Eating Habits
1. Eating out:
   2–4 times per week   3_____
   8–10 times per week   6_____
   More than 10 times per week   10_____

2. Use of salt:
   Little added salt, few salty foods   0_____
   Moderate salt added and/or salty foods   3_____

3. Water:
   Chlorinated water   2_____
   Chlorinated and fluorinated   5_____

4. Chemical stressors (average daily):
   Sugar added to food or drink (1 point per
     5 teaspoons)
   Sweet roll, piece of pie (1 point per item)   _____
   Coke or any regular soft drink (sugar
     content is stressor in this case;
     2 points per can)   _____
   Regular use of white flour (white bread,
     pastries, spaghetti, etc.)   5_____
   Banana split or commercial milk shake   5_____
   Coffee (½ point per cup)   _____
   Tea (½ point per cup)   _____
   Soft drink (1 additional point for caffeine
     consumption, per regular can; ½ point
     for caffeine consumption per diet can)   _____
   Two Anacin® or APC tablets
     (2 points per dose)   _____
   Caffeine benzoate tablets (No-Doze®,
     Vivarin®, etc.; 2 points per dose)   _____

   Eating Habits Subtotal   _____

Alcohol and Drugs (daily consumption)

1. Whiskey, gin, vodka, etc.
   (2 points per ounce) _____
2. Wine (2 points per glass) _____
3. Beer (2 points per can) _____
4. Antidepressant drugs 1_____
5. Tranquilizers 3_____
6. Sleeping pills 3_____
7. Narcotics 5_____
8. Other pain relievers 3_____
9. Cigarettes: 3–10 per day 5_____
   11–20 day 15_____
   21–30 per day 20_____
   31–40 per day 35_____
   More than 40 per day 40_____
   Regular exposure to cigarette smoke of
      someone else for more than 1 hour
      per day 5_____
10. Cigars per day (1 point each) _____
11. Pipefuls of tobacco per day (1 point each) _____

   Alcohol and Drugs Subtotal _____

Physical Activity

1. Adequate exercise (3 days or more
   each week) 0_____
2. Little active physical exercise (1 or 2 days
   per week) 15_____
3. No regular exercise 40_____

   Physical Activity Subtotal _____

Television Watching

1. Per hour per day (2 points) _____

   Television Watching Subtotal _____

Relationships

1. Spend time with friends every week 0_____
2. Active with a group other than at work 0_____

3. Don't have close friends with whom
   I can talk   5_____
4. Not involved in social groups   5_____
5. Married, but moderately unhappy   2_____
6. Married, but very unhappy   5_____
7. Unmarried man over 30   5_____
8. Unmarried woman over 30   2_____

    Relationship Subtotal   _____

Emotional Stress
1. Sleep:
   7–8 hours per day   0_____
   Fewer than 7 hours   3_____
   More than 8 hours   2_____

2. Relaxation:
   Never relax except during sleep   10_____
   Relax or meditate at least 20 minutes
   per day   0_____

3. Weight:
   More than 10 pounds underweight   5_____
   10–15 pounds overweight   5_____
   16–25 pounds overweight   10_____
   26–40 pounds overweight   25_____
   More than 40 pounds overweight   40_____

4. Usual mood:
   Happy, well-adjusted   0_____
   Moderately angry, depressed, or frustrated   10_____
   Very angry, depressed, or frustrated   20_____
   Any other emotional, social, or major stress
   not mentioned—you judge the intensity and
   point value (up to 40 points)   _____

    Emotional Stress Subtotal   _____

Work Stress
1. Sit most of the day   3_____
2. Blue-collar worker   3_____
3. Enjoy work   0_____

4. Mildly frustrated by job   1_____
5. Moderately frustrated by job   3_____
6. Travel overnight more than 1 day per week   5_____
7. Work more than 50 hours per week   10_____
8. Work night shift   5_____
9. No control over work   5_____

Work Stress Subtotal   _____

Safety and Living

1. Live within 10 miles of city of 500,000+   10_____
2. Live within 10 miles of city of 200,000+   5_____
3. Live within 10 miles of city of 50,000+   2_____
4. Live on farm but use pesticides, herbicides,
   chemical fertilizers   10_____
5. Often exceed speed limit   5_____
6. Rarely wear seat belt   5_____
7. Drive under the influence of alcohol or drugs   5_____

Safety and Living Subtotal   _____

Recent Life Changes

1. Death of spouse   100_____
2. Divorce   73_____
3. Marital separation   65_____
4. Jail term   63_____
5. Death of a close family member   63_____
6. Personal injury or illness   53_____
7. Marriage   50_____
8. Fired from job   47_____
9. Marital reconciliation   45_____
10. Retirement   45_____
11. Change in health of family member   44_____
12. Pregnancy   40_____
13. Sex difficulties   39_____
14. Gain of new family member   39_____
15. Business readjustment   39_____
16. Change in financial state   38_____
17. Death of a close friend   37_____
18. Change to a different job or line   36_____
19. Increase arguments with spouse   35_____

20. Mortgage or loan of more than $10,000   31_____
21. Foreclosure of mortgage or loan   30_____
22. Change in responsibilities at work   29_____
23. Son or daughter leaves home   29_____
24. Trouble with in-laws   29_____
25. Outstanding personal achievement   28_____
26. Wife or husband begins or stops work   26_____
27. Begin or end school   26_____
28. Change in living conditions   24_____
29. Revision of personal habits   24_____
30. Trouble with boss   23_____
31. Change in work hours or conditions   20_____
32. Change in residence   20_____
33. Change in schools   20_____
34. Change in recreation   19_____
35. Change in church activities   19_____
36. Change in social activities   18_____
37. Mortgage or loan of less than $10,000   17_____
38. Change in sleeping habits   16_____
39. Change in family gatherings   15_____
40. Change in eating habits   15_____
41. Going on vacation   13_____
42. Christmas holiday season   12_____
43. Minor violations of the law
    (speeding ticket, etc.)   11_____

Add up your Recent Life Changes score.   _____
If your Recent Life Changes score is: _____
Less than 150   0_____
151–250   5_____
251–350   15_____
351 or more   30_____

Recent Life Changes Subtotal   _____

Add Up All Subtotals
   Eating Habits   _____
   Alcohol and Drugs   _____
   Physical Activity   _____
   Television Watching   _____
   Relationships   _____

Emotional Stress   _____
Work Stress   _____
Safety and Living   _____
Recent Life Changes   _____

Total Score   _____

According to the professionals who created this profile, if your total score is less than 25, congratulations. You are living a commendable lifestyle, and you are probably one in ten thousand people. If your total score is 26 to 40, you're still doing well. You probably have a good grasp of health principles; you are experiencing minimum change. Things are basically under control.

If your total score is 41 to 50, you're entering into a risky category; you are taking some chances with your life. There is a fairly strong possibility that the stress in your life may cause physical problems or at least emotional swings. You would do yourself a favor by working to reduce some of the stressors in your life.

If your total score is 50 or more, your life is in the high-risk category; you are physically and emotionally in danger.

Physically you are risking potential heart, lung, and stomach diseases or ailments and stress-induced illness can be fatal. Not all stroke or heart attack victims have a family history of heart disease. Many were simply overloaded on stress.

Emotionally you are a good candidate for stress-induced psychological problems. You should stop at this point and make some immediate plans to reduce your life stressors.

You will quickly see that you have no control in some areas of this evaluation. There is no way to manipulate some stressful circumstances to create a more stabilized environment. If this is the case, begin taking very cautious and gentle care of yourself. Do whatever you can to gain control over as many things as possible, stabilizing your environment.

HOW TO TAKE CARE OF YOURSELF
WHILE ON OVERLOAD

Here are sixteen ways you can reduce your stress load.

1. Get regular and sufficient rest. Go to bed and get up at the same time each day, allowing yourself at least eight hours for rest—even if you can't sleep.
2. Eat properly—three regular meals each day. They don't have to be big meals, but eat with an eye toward proper balance and nutrition.
3. Get regular exercise. If nothing else, go for a half-hour walk each day.
4. Cut back on (quit, if possible) smoking.
5. Take an additional twenty minutes per day for a spiritual quiet time, to pray, meditate, and connect with God. Develop the habit of walking with God. Whenever your mind isn't doing something else, just talk with him. (He doesn't hate you. He loves you and aches while watching his children suffer.) The more you develop your spiritual connection with God, the more ably you will handle your stress load.
6. Cut back on caffeine—coffee, tea, soft drinks.
7. Curtail your use of salt.
8. If you're working at a regular job, limit the number of hours you will give the job in a week. Fifty-five hours should be the top cut-off point. People (especially men) going through divorce frequently attempt to compensate for their bad feelings by overdosing on work.
9. If you have kids at home, stay as closely connected to them as you can. Emotional distance from your kids during your divorce will only add to everyone's stress levels.
10. Stay away from making long-term decisions. Though some decisions may be thrust upon you, try not to make major career changes to move to another city or make major financial transactions. If you must make a big decision, talk it over with someone who knows you well. Listen carefully. Someone less emotionally involved with the situation may bring a more rational viewpoint to your decision.
11. Don't date! (We'll talk more about this late in the book.)
12. Spend time, as much social time as you're able, with same-sex friends.

13. Take some vacation time if you can.
14. Develop a new hobby or interest of some sort, to keep yourself fresh.
15. Do nice things for yourself, just to make yourself happy. Some people love bubble baths. Others enjoy bicycle riding or walking in the woods. Buy some flowers for yourself and put them in a vase in your kitchen. Do something every day just to be nice to yourself.
16. Either become or remain connected to some form of Christian fellowship, where you find support, prayer, and caring. Churches are supposed to be good places for healing a broken heart or life. If your church is not, find one that is.

Even if you feel like putting your head to the wall and dying, stop right now and do one thing to take care of yourself. Just the fact that you're reading this book is a sign of hope. You are a survivor.

REDUCING STRESS IN YOUR RELATIONSHIPS

Stress and Your Ex-Spouse

As you might imagine, you will probably not enjoy a stress-free relationship with your ex-spouse for some time to come. In fact, you might never again be with that person without experiencing some degree of stress.

Consequently, it is wise to do everything in your power to lower the stress level in that relationship.

The quality of the relationship you have with your ex-spouse will be in direct correlation to the number of and energy behind games and battles that each person brings to it. These games include:

- withholding, underpaying, or paying late on child support checks;
- ongoing suits or countersuits regarding children or property;
- scheduling conflicting activities for the children when the

ex-spouse is supposed to have them for regular visitation;

- accusations of child abuse;
- telephone harassment;
- calling complaints to the ex-spouse's employer;
- entering the ex-spouse's home or apartment, after divorce, to "retrieve" property;
- using the social network to spread hatred toward one's ex-spouse.

Almost anything can be used as a weapon: money, children, friends, property, church, job. You name it.

These ongoing battles or games appear to have the goal of reducing, or getting even with, the ex-spouse. The grand deception, however, is that they actually *keep the couple attached*.

Hatred is not the opposite of love. Ask any therapist. Indifference is the opposite of love. Hatred has been described as a reverse side of the coin the front side of which is love. It's all one coin, and the "value" of the coin is *attachment*. Battles, games, manipulation, control issues, all have the effect of keeping divorcing individuals *in* a relationship. It may be a horribly bad relationship, but it's still a connection.

Why might people want to remain involved with their ex-spouse via games, battles, or other measures? Here are a few common reasons:

- unreadiness to face being single; fear of being alone;
- religious beliefs that divorce is always wrong, which prompt people to attempt to stay married or remarry at any cost;
- avoidance of dealing with rejection or failure;
- blind competitiveness;
- self-pity;
- "for the sake of the children";
- bitterness.

One can be so driven by any of these issues (and others), that an individual simply refuses to let go of the ex-spouse. For some, even a desperately negative and bitter relationship is better than no relationship at all. It sounds distorted, and it is, but it is true for many.

As for your situation: *You can't control the games your ex may wish to play. You can only control your own responses and your role in the games.* You have the ability to control at least your side of the equation.

You're not necessarily "deescalating" the game to make things nice and happy for your ex-spouse. For right now, just do it for yourself, to be able to eat and sleep better. Seek peace. That doesn't mean you have to become a doormat. You can retain your individual rights and self-respect and still work toward peace.

Stress and Your In-laws

Another relationship that may cause you no small amount of stress during your divorce is with your in-laws. In many cases these relationships have been loving and supportive, and it's hard to know what to do now that the family has split apart.

There is no right way to deal with people with whom one was once attached through marriage. Probably the best tack is that which seems most natural and healing. If the in-laws still want to be close to you, think it through and decide what that will mean in your life. You may wish it, or you may not. If they decide it would be better if you just dropped out of their lives, that may be the best course.

Don't force any issues. Don't make them choose between loving you and loving your ex-spouse. (You will probably lose.) Be patient. With time, some of the hurt will pass. If there was a loving relationship before divorce, it might be restored eventually.

If there are children involved, there are those "special" relationships to consider: grandparents, uncles, aunts, and cousins. Children usually want to have ongoing relationships with their relatives, and there is often a unique bond between grandparent and grandchild. Yet if the in-laws treat the children with disrespect, anger, or bitterness or seem to drag the divorce and its issues into the ongoing relationship (especially if it's harmful or destructive to you or the children), it may be better to quietly and gracefully spend less time, or no time, with them.

Divorce is stressful enough. Why complicate it more by forcing a relationship with in-laws if that very relationship adds to the stress? Take some time out. Either side can always renew a relationship at some future point, but during the months right before and after divorce, it may be less stressful to take a breather.

On the other hand, if they can handle it, if you can handle it, and if love remains, then enjoy the relationship.

STRESS AND COPING MECHANISMS

Carl Jung is credited with saying, "Neurosis is always a substitute for legitimate suffering." As a person's stress and pain escalate, it is normal for him or her to search for some "thing," maybe an activity or relationship, that can help reduce the pain, anxiety, or stress. One just wants to pull the cork from the bottle to release the pressure.

Sometimes that's the best one can do—just hang on and survive for a while. But the more one uses his or her coping mechanism, the more it becomes a fixture in one's life.

Imagine purchasing a gerbil. With the pet comes a small wire-mesh cage, a watering bottle, a little food bowl, and, of course, the exercise wheel. Let's focus on the exercise wheel, and take an imaginative leap: You have somehow become the gerbil.

It's not much of a life, although your daily needs for food and water are met. Day after day you sit in this stupid cage and watch as life passes you by.

One day you try the exercise wheel. Seems to work pretty well. You have a good run. You jump off the wheel, panting. *Phew! Good workout! Think I'll try that again tomorrow.*

Tomorrow comes, and so does the anxiety of spending another day in the cage. You get on the wheel and run. It feels good and although you're not getting anywhere, you know you're burning off some energy; your anxiety level seems to be lower after a good "wheel run."

Soon you learn that when you're feeling anxious or

stressful about anything, you can get on the wheel and run until your paws are pink. Then you don't feel bad anymore—for a while, anyway. And when you do start feeling bad again, you can just jump on the old wheel and run it off.

The wheel is the gerbil's coping mechanism. Here's how it works: Though a coping mechanism doesn't help you get anywhere, it does help you get rid of some stress, anxiety, or pain. For a while. Until the stress, anxiety, or pain mounts to an intolerable level again. Frequently, this "intolerable level" is subconscious; you don't really know why you need to use the wheel—your coping mechanism. You just feel that urge and desire the release.

Divorce frequently leads people to find or create coping mechanisms. Almost anything can be a coping mechanism. Some people use food to feel good—for a while. Some people turn to exercise and become fitness freaks with fantastic bodies. Currently this is a highly acceptable way of burning off stress, pain, or anxiety.

Some become compulsive workaholics, spendaholics, or sexaholics. Some go on for advanced academic degrees. Some lose themselves in the world of television or videos.

Probably the most common coping mechanism is the Novocain of another intimate relationship. Pay special attention to the word *Novocain*.

When one goes to a dentist for a filling, the dentist deadens the nerves around the tooth so you don't feel the pain.

When pain is not part of a marriage being ripped apart, it is frequently because one or both partners are using the Novocain of another intimate relationship. One doesn't have to hurt when that hurt is being assuaged within the tender support of a new, loving relationship.

Another mechanism frequently used to dull or avoid the pain of divorce is that of chemical abuse—drinking too much, frequent use of prescription drugs such as amphetamines or barbiturates or other mood-altering (but "safe," because the doctor prescribed them) drugs. Some people turn to street drugs such as marijuana or cocaine to avoid the pain of divorce.

Using drugs to numb emotional pain is similar to using

Novocain to "cure" an abscessed tooth. Its numbing effects are temporary.

Some divorcing people fill all their free hours with bridge groups, tennis, singles' organizations, trips, dances, and the like. The (usually unconscious) mental process that drives this form of avoidance goes something like this: *Whenever I'm alone I find myself thinking about the divorce and feeling absolutely rotten. So! Presto! I just won't be alone. I'll keep myself so busy that I never have time to think about the divorce, and then I won't feel rotten.* It does work—again about as well as using Novocain to cure an abscessed tooth.

Some coping mechanisms have positive side effects. A person may need exercise to reduce weight and tone up the ol' body. And pouring on the midnight oil may get someone to the top of the corporation.

But coping mechanisms usually don't bring emotional health and lasting peace. They treat the symptoms rather than the "disease." And coping mechanisms are almost always counterproductive to good, healthy, intimate relationships. The exercise freak may eventually find that he or she can't stay in close, long-term relationships. It's not because of the exercising; it's because the exercising has become a way to escape the pain of relationships; relational skills have been left to die. The workaholic may have risen to the top of the corporate pile, but the relationships "sacrificed" on the way up tell a tale of a dysfunctional personality, incapable of holding intimate relationships over an extended period.

The point is this: As you suffer through divorce, as you wade through the junk, the emotions, the anxiety, as you struggle to balance your stressed-out life, don't do too much "wheel work." That is, if you are doing anything compulsively or "too much," you are probably using it as a way to escape from the stress and anxiety you face. Don't let yourself get hooked on "numb-ers." They help numb the pain, like magic, but it's not necessarily healthy. There's a reason for pain of a broken heart, just as there's reason for the pain of a broken leg.

The higher the stress load, the more seductive the coping mechanisms, the "wheels" of life. Recognize that they may help you feel better for a while, but they don't get you anywhere. On the other side of the coin, they are usually *counterproductive* to what you really need: love, acceptance, trust, healing, and affirmation.

Think of a Novocain-numbed mouth that cannot feel the pain of the dentist's drill. Neither can it feel the soft touch of a loving hand or the caress of a child. That mouth is numb. Period.

JUST HOLD ON

At the beginning of this chapter I described a friend who'd gone coo-coo—having been hit on the head. He was repeating basic questions over and over.

If you're feeling stressed out, go ahead, ask questions. They provide a framework within which you can begin to reorder your shattered life. They help you put new pieces in place, where old relationships and old answers have been ripped away. Ask as many questions as you need to ask and keep on asking them even if you feel you're making a fool of yourself.

But know that you probably won't find many answers of much help during the first six months to a year after your separation or divorce. Actually, answers to questions are not what you really need at this time. That is to say, if God himself came and sat with you in your living room and gave you an answer to every question you have, you'd still hurt. In fact, you may never discover all the answers, but keep asking as long as you need to.

Several years ago one of my daughters had a broken arm. As she recovered, she was sore for weeks. Immediately after the break, even if I could have answered all her medical questions, the pain would still have remained. So ask as many questions as you need to—to begin to reorient yourself to your new circumstances, but don't assume any answers will erase the pain. Just let it hurt for a while. You *will* get better. For now, take your time. Heal slowly, from the inside out. Learn (or relearn) how to tap the amazing love and healing of Jesus Christ.

QUESTIONS FOR REFLECTION

1. What's your Lifestyle Profile score?

2. Besides divorce, what other "big pieces" of your life are in chaos? (The purpose of this question is to help you identify reasons why you may feel crazy, out of control, or stressed out.)

3. Review the list of ways to take care of yourself while on overload. Which will be most helpful to you? Which, if any, are you willing to implement?

4. If you are under heavy stress and not willing to make any lifestyle changes, try to determine why. Is it because your life is truly out of control? Or is there another, hidden reason? If so, what?

5. How do stress, your ex-spouse, and your in-laws, interact in your life at this moment? How can you reduce your own stress levels in these relationships?

6. If you have children, how are they communicating their stress levels? What behavior tells you they're under heavy stress?

7. What coping mechanisms are you using? How are they helping you get by? How might they become counter-productive to relationships in the future?

8. What two objectives do you hope to attain as you progress through this book and recover from your divorce?

ACTION ITEMS

1. If you're in a small group or divorce-recovery program and are using this book as a guide, review the Group Ground Rules on page 15. Be conversant with them before the next group meeting.

2. If you have not already done so, and if you're in a small group or divorce-recovery group, establish a regular meeting time and place for the next several weeks.

3. Whether you're in a group or not, make a sign, as big or small as you wish, as pretty or as plain: TAKE ONE DAY AT A TIME. Place the sign where you will see it at least twice each day.

4. Write down three ways you can begin to reduce your overall stress score—this week. Step out and take

action. As you attempt to reduce your stress level, write down your emotional response. What happens inside you?

5. Write down three coping mechanisms you as a child saw your parents using. Write a few paragraphs regarding how their use of these coping mechanisms affected your life.
6. Write down three coping mechanisms you currently use. How do they compare with the coping mechanisms your parents used?
7. If you have children, write down three coping mechanisms you see in your children. Compare these items with the three you saw in your own parents and the three you use. What similarities do you see? What impact do you think your coping mechanisms may have upon the lives of your children?
8. Write four paragraphs describing how your coping mechanisms help you avoid dealing with the stress, anxiety, and pain of your life. As you write, reflect upon what life would be like if you did not resort to the coping mechanism. Reflect upon how these coping mechanisms might keep you from experiencing the joys and happiness of life.

FOR SPIRITUAL GROWTH

1. How does the stress of your life interact with your relationship with God? Does it drive you toward him or away from him? Why?
2. How do the coping mechanisms of your life interact with your ability to trust God?
3. Read Romans 8:38–39. Do you believe that nothing (absolutely nothing in the world) can separate you from the love of God, or do you think that divorce is an "unforgivable" sin? If you believe that divorce is unforgivable, how do you justify that perspective as you read this text? How well are you connecting with the love of God right now? In what way would you be able to accept any expression of love from God?

4. Read and reflect upon this meditation, "Footprints."

One night a man had a dream. He dreamed he was walking along the beach with the LORD. Across the sky flashed scenes from his life. For each scene, he noticed two sets of footprints in the sand; one belonging to him, and the other to the LORD.

When the last scene of his life flashed before him, he looked back at the footprints in the sand. He noticed that many times along the path of his life there was only one set of footprints. He also noticed that it happened at the very lowest and saddest times in his life.

This really bothered him and he questioned the LORD about it. "LORD, you said that once I decided to follow you, you'd walk with me all the way. But I have noticed that during the most troublesome times in my life there is only one set of footprints. I don't understand why when I needed you most you would leave me."

The LORD replied, "My precious, precious child, I love you and I would never leave you. During your times of trial and suffering, when you see only one set of footprints, it was then that I carried you."

Author Unknown

‡

CHAPTER 4

HOW DID WE GET WHERE WE ARE?

Abraham Lincoln once said, "If we could first know where we were, and whither we are tending, we could better judge what to do, and how to do it."

Most people recovering from divorce find it helpful to have a clear picture of where things went wrong. With this new understanding you are better able to work through your emotions, your grief, and walk into the future with confidence that you won't make the same mistakes again.

A week hardly passes without someone coming into my office saying, "I can't believe I married another alcoholic." Or, "My first wife was so dependent on me, for everything. I can't believe I married another person just like her." Or, "My first husband was such a controlling person. I hated it. And now I'm dating another guy who is just as bad, if not worse. What's wrong?"

Let's go back to the beginning and consider the reasons you married. Do any of these sound familiar?

- fear of being single forever;
- deep feelings of low self-esteem;
- anger toward parents and subsequent desire to leave home;

- fear of facing college or high school graduation and not being married; fear of missing the largest "pool" of marriage candidates, one's classmates;
- wild desire for an immediate romantic connection with a "dream baby";
- pregnancy or feelings of guilt regarding sexual involvement;
- parental pressure to marry;
- fear of financial insecurity;
- desire to fill the emptiness you felt in your spirit.

People who marry for these kinds of reasons often have an excessive emotional need to be connected with someone else, in hopes that this "other" will provide a sense of internal stability.

The greater one's "need" to be married, the more undeveloped the sense of self. If I need you to make me feel good about me, then I'm not comfortable with who I am.

If someone can't "do life" without a spouse, then that person probably can't "do life" with a spouse either. The broken *part* of your personality, that which requires someone else to "pump you up" if you're to feel good about yourself, will not be fixed by marriage. That from which you are running when running into the arms of a relationship will eventually, and certainly, catch up with you again and cause problems in marriage.

But what went wrong that you might have been such a needy person in the first place? Let's look at a few examples of codependent couples—the needs they brought with them to the marriage and how these needs contributed to their divorce.

You may not like the term *codependency*, which is often associated with alcoholism; the alcoholic needs someone to "balance" his [or her] alcoholism by "taking care" of him, allowing him the luxury of being drunk and irresponsible, either controlling him or being controlled by him.

But the concept of one person being dependent upon another person in an unhealthy and dysfunctional manner has now moved far beyond the realm of alcoholism. *Codependency* has, in fact, become a buzzword within therapeutic circles, because it provides helpful insight into why people keep falling into the same "hole" again and again. Oh, it probably didn't look like a "hole" at the time. In fact, it probably looked like a pretty good choice—and there lies the blindness of codependency, which works like this: "I have needs that make me the kind of person who attracts another kind of person whose specific needs interlock with mine."

HIGH-PERFORMANCE, HIGH-MAINTENANCE CODEPENDENCY

In college Bill was the life of the party and Nancy was his cohort. People used to look at them and shake their heads! What a team!

Bill was six-two; a football quarterback with blond hair, green eyes, broad shoulders, square chin—and highly intelligent. Always a winner, he felt he deserved the best in life, which included the most popular girl on campus—Nancy, slender, five-foot-nine, stunningly beautiful, homecoming queen.

Nancy could hardly believe her good fortune. What a catch. After all, she'd grown up "on empty" at home, not getting much attention from her parents. Her father had been gone much of the time, and her mother had been busy climbing her own social ladder. Nancy just wanted to be loved and here was Bill, who seemed to love her very much. She "leaned" on him, drawing from his strength and vitality, and he wore her on his arm like a bauble.

Ten years later, after they'd had two "perfect" children, Bill left Nancy for another woman. Nancy was crushed and confused. What had happened? Well, Bill had discovered that wearing a bauble on his arm wasn't enough. Since he "deserved the best life had to offer," he left when he found someone "better" than Nancy, whose dependence and "clinging" spirit was weighing him down. You see, relationships built upon need (his for a trophy and hers for a pillar of strength and love) are houses of cards just waiting for the right wind to blow them down. Codependent relationships are built upon need, hunger, "empty cups," and weakness, rather than upon mutual strength, affection, respect, and individual wholeness.

ISOLATED-LONER AND WARM-HEARTED-RESCUER CODEPENDENCY

Bud had never known what it felt like to be loved. Struggling with a decaying marriage, his parents hadn't had the time or energy to meet Bud's needs. Donna's home life had been chaotic, too. A military career man, her dad had been transferred every twelve to eighteen months. She'd never had a chance to sink roots in a community.

Bud, who didn't have the skills and the information to connect meaningfully with anyone, married Donna, who had no ability or skills to connect with her own feelings (and therefore was attracted to someone who "needed" her).

Donna had learned that she could get many of her needs met if she helped other people meet theirs. She was constantly involved with this and that "stray puppy," as she could feel and even soothe that person's pain. Hurting people—including Bud—flocked to her.

But in time Donna was telling Bud exactly what he was feeling. So Bud learned to keep to himself, especially his emotions. He became so separated from his emotions that he felt nothing other than vague anger and loneliness.

Bud grew increasingly disenchanted with know-it-all Donna, and Donna grew so frustrated with silent Bud until one day they split, each blaming the other.

(After their breakup, Donna found another wounded soul to whom to attach, and Bud found another woman who thought she could rescue him. That's what codependency does.)

ALCOHOLIC CODEPENDENT SYSTEM

Sally grew up with an alcoholic father. If she didn't walk on eggshells, Dad would explode like a hand grenade. She left home as soon as she was able and married Dave, whose father was a workaholic, always gone from the home, always "too busy." Before the wedding Sally saw that Dave had a temper, but she was used to making excuses for her father; she never confronted Dave's anger. Actually, she had learned her "enabler" pattern by watching her mother handle her father when drunk. She'd call the office and tell the boss that her husband was sick again. So when Dave yelled at their children, Sally made excuses: "He's just under a lot of pressure, kids. We'll have to be real careful of what we say around him." (Sally was teaching her children just as her mother taught her.)

This went on for several years. Dave's anger toward Sally increased as he lost respect for her, seeing her grovel. Sally's repressed anger increased to the point that she suffered from perforated ulcers. One day one of them said to the other, "I don't love you anymore. I'm not sure I ever did. I want a divorce."

After a few months' separation and a half-hearted attempt at counseling, they divorced. Sally got the kids except for one weekend a month. Dave hates paying child support but does so grudgingly. They had to sell the house and split up the estate.

A COMMON THREAD

What common thread runs through these stories? Let's start with their courting days, when halos graced their heads. He "saw" an angel in her, and she helped polish the halo to help him believe in angels. She "saw" an officer and a gentleman in him, and he polished the halo to help her believe in officers and gentlemen.

Back then a shimmering globe surrounded them, keeping others out of the relationship. No matter what anyone outside the globe said to the people inside the globe (Can you live with his temper? Can you live with her mood swings? He sure seems to drink a lot, doesn't he? She has a history of promiscuity; do you think she can be true to you? She seems to be pretty timid about life, can you live with it?), the answer was always, "Oh, yes, of course I know that. In fact, we've talked about it, and we're sure it can be resolved."

Then came the wedding day, when friends and relatives gathered to witness the vows. The "honeymoon" lasted months (or years) and the relationship settled into a predictable pattern, becoming hardened in the cement of its own history, with mutual expectations and roles established and lived out.

As time passed, the passion of youth faded and the greater need for deep, mature adult intimacy emerged.

But the baggage that each partner brought from childhood continued to live a life of its own. It must be said, parenthetically, that *all* people bring unresolved past issues into their marriages. Everyone brings hurts, memories, and patterns that may or may not cause marital difficulties. When husband and wife work hard at relating to each other, communicating openly with each other, trusting each other with their deepest parts, and maturing both relationally and spiritually, those unresolved issues can provide meaningful and productive avenues for personal, relational, and spiritual growth. This frequently occurs in good marriages, providing even deeper levels of love, intimacy, and connectedness.

But as partners "resolved" things in ways that hurt each other or themselves, they resolved nothing. Rather than standing side by side and facing issues together, as they had when courting, they began to let things slip a little. They began to feel separated from each other. They suspected that the other person wasn't working as hard on the relationship as *they* were working. They began to keep score.

They found one, then two, and soon several small issues that had been left unattended for too long, which began to gain that insidious "life of their own." Maybe none of the issues was worth a major confrontation, yet together they formed a formidable barrier between the partners.

It's not as if either partner was thinking of divorce or even separation at this point of unresolved issues. But when too many conflicts were left unaddressed, when skills for resolving problems were limited, then a wedge formed between them.

At some point in the relationships at least one of the partners became aware that the unresolved small problems had become a major problem. This major problem involved major pieces of each spouse's personality, coupled with issues from childhood.

The rift of emotional distance deepened, whether suddenly or slowly. Trust waned. As both parties banked less on the marriage, both became emotionally vulnerable, tentatively at first, but as the emotional separation increased, so did the vulnerability and their opposing, defensive positions.

At some point one or both partners said, "Enough is enough! I've had it with you! No more!" and decided physically to withdraw from the other party. The precipitating factor might have been a major fight, another bout with a drunken partner, another affair, another beating, or it might have been a quiet recognition that the relationship was dead. One person physically moved out—or kicked the other out.

The separation was an act of hopeless frustration: "I can't figure out how to handle this marriage anymore." But as the separation was prolonged, as the issues precipitating it were left unaddressed and additional issues were added to fuel the fire, the chances for reconciliation dwindled. *What went wrong? Why can't we fix it?* Still unable to work through the dysfunctional relationship, the marriages ended in divorce.

THE PAST LEAKS INTO THE PRESENT

Many components set up a person for a codependent relationship, and nearly all are tied to one's childhood home. Do you see any of your childhood patterns in this list:

1. Alcoholism almost anywhere within the family system (parent, sibling, uncle, aunt, grandparent, cousin).
2. Any form of chemical addiction within the family system.
3. Dysfunctional family system:
   - father unemployed much of the time;
   - lots of anger, yelling, blaming, etc.;
   - an unpredictable parent with strong mood swings;
   - a chronically ill parent (unpredictable, unavailable, or the cause of foreboding or fear);
   - an absent parent—or divorce;
   - parent with serious mental disorders;
   - family system in which children experienced any substantial or repetitive chaos threatening their sense of well-being or safety.
4. Workaholism on the part of either parent.

5. Excessive rigidity (often in the form of excessive religious fervor or racial intolerance) on the part of one or both parents.
6. Any form of parental abuse against the child, including emotional (frequent harsh words said to hurt the child), physical (beating with belts, razor straps, wooden rods, slapping in the face, etc.), or sexual abuse.
7. Parents setting impossibly high or unrealistic standards for children (always damaging, but especially damaging when parents used harsh punishment as motivator for children's lack of attainment of these impossibly high or unrealistic standards).
8. Scapegoating—one parent becoming too attached to one child, giving that child too much power within the family system; playing that parent/child combination against the other parent.
9. Emotional unavailability of one or both parents. In *Christian Men Who Hate Women*, Margaret Rinck says, "Neglecting children's basic needs has the same effect as if they were physically abandoned. No one is there for the children at an emotional level. The children are in some way on their own."

The more deeply one has been wounded, the higher the probability that one will be codependent. The pain from the past leaks into the present. The picture is not hard to see: A child grows up in a family system that causes damage so the child is unable to form normal, close-in, trusting, peaceful relationships. The child is "damaged goods." The child's "relational con-necters" are bent or broken. The child does not enter adulthood with the capability of (a) good relational selections (choosing emotionally healthy people with whom to be friends, people who are not themselves "damaged goods") and (b) bringing to relationships sufficient personal strength to maintain *healthy* relationships.

Some theorists believe that people tend to marry spouses who are most like, or most opposite to, the parent with whom they have the most unresolved issues. These "unresolved issues" lead one to attempt to replicate the parental relationship, *or* completely avoid anything that resembles the parental relationship. These are separation and differentiation issues; the more unresolved issues that remain between parent and child, the greater the likelihood of adult relational problems. The "child" has not yet "separated" from childhood issues with Mom and/or Dad and consequently has not separated from Mom and/or Dad.

To be more specific, codependent relationships include these elements:

1. An agreement that says, "I'll use you for what I need, and you use me for what you need; I'll lean on you and you lean on me."
2. Strong emotional needs being acted out (strong attachment-hunger, strong fear of abandonment, strong need for control or dependence).
3. Some element of the sense that "something bigger than both of us is going on here."
4. Frequently a sense that one "knows" the other person better than one realistically could.
5. Frequently a sense that one is somehow responsible for the feelings of the other person.

ISN'T EVERYONE CODEPENDENT?

It's a legitimate question. Doesn't virtually every close, trusting, sharing, open relationship include elements of codependency?

The answer is yes. As we draw closer to people, we begin to draw a certain degree of self-esteem from them; we "lean" toward them for support and affirmation and feel a certain level of responsibility for their feelings if we say or do things that are unkind or hurtful.

Yet it's a matter of degree and substance. How *much* does one lean upon the other person and for what reasons? How much of one's "relational weight" does one place upon the other person, or how much of the other person's weight does one try to carry? How "empty" is either partner, and how much does either believe he or she can "fill" the other? How desperate is the "leaning" upon the other? What would happen if the other momentarily pulled away? Would there be a sudden "crash" accompanied with deep anger and hurt, or would there be *acceptance* and allowance for the other's need for some "space"?

While it's normal for a married couple to be closely knitted, for them to operate as a "team" in many situations, and for them to feel responsible for caring for and nurturing each other, it is also normal and healthy for each to take full responsibility for his or her own life, to stand on one's own two feet and walk forward into life without having to lean against the partner. These two simple diagrams depict healthy versus codependent relationships:

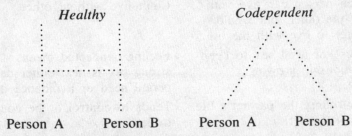

In the healthy relationship, both partners basically stand up straight, not heavily leaning against each other, but walking side by side. Both partners get most of their "supplies" from a variety of sources, most significant of which is the "inside" source: one's own self-esteem. The healthy partners are more able to stand on their own strength and reach out to the other partner, as shown in the diagram by the dots drawn between the two healthy partners.

In the codependent relationship, both partners lean heavily against the other; they know no other way; it's what they feel to be normal. If one party moves, the other falls, so they both need (and in their own ways attempt to control, overtly or covertly) the other party. Both partners attempt to get most of their "supplies" from their codependent partner, as their meaningful contacts with the rest of the world are limited or nonexistent. They "lean" so much that each is unable to "make it" without the other.

HEALTHY VERSUS CODEPENDENT RELATIONSHIPS

Sometimes it's helpful to see comparisons between healthy and codependent relationships. The following list is not original in content, but something I've pulled together over a long time, from scores of conversations and sources. Healthy relationships have boundaries. Each person is whole, separate from the other, and comfortable with that separateness.

Healthy Relationships	Unhealthy Relationships
Takes time to develop	Happens fast, sometimes almost instantly
Each person can live without the other, but would prefer to live with the other	Can't live without other
Does not need sex to keep relationship growing	Feeling connected means strong sex issues, either desperate need or avoidance of
Controlling the partner's life is not a priority	Tends to control or be controlled
Harbors few thoughts of the other person being "the ideal person" for me	Thinks often of the other person being "the ideal person" for me
Bases relationship primarily on friendship	Bases relationship primarily upon need
Is willing to give up short-term pleasures for long-term gains	Is not willing to give up short-term pleasures for long-term gains
Surrounds self with several healthy relationships; not starved for close-in friendships	Is usually isolated from other healthy relationships, creating need for the "one" special relationship
Has resolved most childhood issues and is at peace with self and world	Carries past hurts forward into future relationships and is not at peace with self and world

Healthy Relationships	Unhealthy Relationships
Possesses overall sense of peace, maturity, and stability	Overall sense of being driven, instability and deep "desire"; overall sense of relationship being all-consuming
Allows for independence and individuality	Does not allow for independence or individuality; threatened by partner's personal growth
Allows for both oneness and separateness from the other person	Recognizes few if any ego boundaries: "We are one"; "We know each other without knowing how we know"
Freely asks for what is needed	Depends on the other person "knowing" what is needed; plays psychological and social games to get needs met
Encourages self-sufficiency of both partners	Needs the other in order to feel complete
Can live with flaws and gives unconditional love	Cannot live with or tolerate flaws and demands unconditional love
Possesses personal sense of self-worth and self-esteem	Looks to the other for affirmation and worth
Is able to care for the other, yet with appropriate detachment	Cannot detach from the other and feels responsible for the other person's feelings
Handles feelings as they come, deals with them spontaneously, without dragging old issues into present situations	Reconnects with old, negative feelings, brings them to play in present situations
Bases relationship on mutual integrity	Bases relationship on many power games:

Healthy Relationships	Unhealthy Relationships
	• giving advice or orders • putting down the partner • smothering or overnurturing the other • setting up one partner as superior, one inferior • making decisions for the other • desiring to change the other; unwilling to change self • needing to win or be right • being aggressively assertive • being stubbornly resistant to change; set in own ways • being verbally, physically, or sexually abusive
Experiences true intimacy, based on relational depth	Experiences pseudo intimacy, based on sexual involvement and/or a quick sense of vulnerability
Is comfortable with commitment	Is fearful of commitment, primarily afraid of one's own ability to make and sustain long-term commitment
Is able to let go when relationship is not good or healthy	Fears letting go (abandonment issues)
Gives from sense of freedom and desire to share	Gives in order to get
Usually comes from home in which child felt loved, supported, nurtured, and unconditionally accepted	Usually comes from home in which child did not feel loved, supported, nurtured, and unconditionally accepted

Healthy Relationships	Unhealthy Relationships
Usually felt safe and protected as a child, in spite of any home chaos	Usually is a product of somewhat chaotic home life in which child did not feel safe and protected
Is usually able to control emotions; when emotions are strong, is usually still able to make solid decisions without hurting others	Frequently experiences loss of emotional control: the stronger the emotion, the more out of control and more prone to hurting others this person will be
Sees self as being basically in control of own life and circumstances	Sees others and external circumstances as being in control of life
Does not use blame as a tool to avoid responsibility	Often uses blame to avoid responsibility
Grew up with very little shame-based motivation	Is frequently highly "shame bound" due to frequent use of shame as motivational or correctional tool during childhood
Can live with or without sex for long periods of time with very little change in relationship	Cannot live without sex for very long without some substantial change in relationship
Tends to look at all relationships realistically, without idealizing or castigating	Tends to "idealize" people, putting some on pedestals and making villains of others
Is comfortable with aloneness	Is not comfortable with aloneness

A LOOK BACKWARDS

Divorce is always a two-person event.

After reading this list, ask the big question: What was it like being married to you?

Were you a tyrant? Were you a little gray mouse hiding in a corner? Were you a hand grenade that went off every once in a while? Were you a clingy piece of spaghetti? Were you an emotional/relational void? Were you a roller coaster?

If you saw a substantial number of right-hand-column issues in yourself or your relationships ask yourself, "What's bent and broken in *me*? What part did I have in this marital disaster?"

One of the most critical questions to ask regarding one's own divorce, is "Why did *I* select *that* person to marry?" It's useless to blame the ex-spouse, calling him or her a "jerk" or an "alcoholic" or a "cheat." The only helpful question is "Why did I select that person? What did I see in him or her? What attracted me? What strength? What weakness? To what vulnerability, perceived strength, or other personal characteristic did I attach? What made that person, above all others, appealing to me? What about me attracted him or her? What did I do to "draw in" that person? How did that person "fill me up" where I was empty? How did that person make me "whole"?

Take a close look at that last question. How can *any other* person *ever* make anyone else whole? That need for wholeness is a core issue in codependent relationships.

Let God Fill the Void

T. S. Elliot wrote a poem called "The Hollow Men," acknowledging the emptiness of the human spirit. No one was perfectly nurtured and supported by a parent, so as to feel complete and whole. Saint Augustine said that in each person there is a God-shaped void. Though we try to fill it with work or personal relationships, or love from another human, it can never be filled—except by the Spirit of God.

God, the One who created you uniquely, the One who knew you before you were born (see Ps. 139), has said that he would place his Spirit within his children: "I will give them an undivided heart and put a new spirit in them; I will remove from them their heart of stone and give them a heart of flesh" (Ezek. 11:19).

That's a wonderful promise, and turning to him, asking him

to be at the center of your life is the starting point of your healing. No human can ever totally satisfy your need or make you whole.

But I Feel So Bad

This chapter has no doubt churned up a great deal of guilt in your life—especially if you saw yourself as the "innocent" party in your divorce. Take heart. The next chapter walks you through the process of coming to terms with your guilt. Yes, you may carry responsibility, but you don't have to carry that burden for the rest of your life. The night may be dark, but morning is coming.

QUESTIONS FOR REFLECTION

1. What codependent characteristics do you see in your own life?
2. Why is it impossible for a seriously codependent person to (a) establish and (b) maintain intimate relationships? (*Intimate* does not here imply *sexual*. To link intimacy with sex-issues is often a form of codependency.)
3. With hindsight, list some of the characteristics that formed the codependencies of your marriage. How did you link up with your ex? Why did your relationship fail?
4. Why do people often fall into the same hole again, after struggling so hard to get out of the last one? Why can't people see what they're getting into in new relationships?
5. Try to identify any damaging experiences, patterns, or themes from your *childhood*, that played out in your marriage.

ACTION ITEMS

1. List all the characteristics of codependency that apply to yourself. Be as thorough as you can, filling as many notebook pages as you need.

2. Read over the list, and write a few paragraphs describing how it would have been to be married to a person just like yourself. Be creative and be as perceptive about yourself as you can.

3. Use the list again and explore how some of those "pieces" got built into your personality. From where did they come? How would an intelligent and resourceful person such as yourself go about making corrections in those "pieces"?

4. Educate yourself. Some wonderful books about codependency are available. Look at the list of books at the end of the book. Begin with Melody Beattie's *Codependent No More*, and branch out from there. There's no reason for you to be stuck for the rest of your life in the same cycle, with the same kinds of unfulfilling relationships.

FOR SPIRITUAL GROWTH

1. Read John 8:1–11. Why do you think Christ didn't condemn the woman in this story? How did he give her the strength to go and begin a new life? What strength would you wish to receive from God if you could get it?

2. Read John 4:1–26. Was this woman able to hide her dysfunctional personality from Jesus? How did he react? What did he offer her—to fill the void in her life?

‡

CHAPTER 5

WALKING THROUGH GUILT

I felt so guilty. The unthinkable had happened: My marriage had failed. Now my children were going to grow up in a divorced home; I had breached my own value system in getting divorced; I wondered if God could ever accept me. I even felt guilty about looking forward to a new lease on life.

There are many potential themes of guilt within divorce. Here are just a few:

I probably could have worked harder at the marriage to make it work. Now that it's done, I look back and feel guilty that I didn't try harder.

I feel relieved now that it's over, and yet I feel guilty about feeling relieved.

My kids are a constant ache within my heart. I know they love both my ex and me, and now they're going to grow up in a broken home. I feel fearful for them and guilty for being part of their pain.

I was so mean, so petty during our marriage. I now look at what I did to cause the divorce and feel guilty about it.

Divorce was always something that happened to other people, not to nice Christians like myself. Now I'm divorced, and I feel so guilty before God.

My life was a gift from God, and now I've made a wreckage of it. I feel guilty for having been a part of the destruction.

We got married for all the wrong reasons—we were immature, sexually out of control, infatuated—we should never have married. Now I feel guilty for marrying and for divorcing, too!

My parents have really been hurt through my divorce. I feel guilty when I'm with them.

From almost the very start it was apparent that we didn't have the maturity to make a marriage work. We almost hated each other at times, and still I feel guilty for not having the strength to make the marriage work.

I feel as if I've let down everyone I love.

This divorce has been so much more sad and hurtful than I thought it would ever be. I feel guilty for all the pain everyone's experienced because of it.

Each individual has personally tailored guilt response when going through divorce. The only thing that might come close to being "standard" or usual is that most divorcing people experience some guilt, varying from mild to devastating.

A DEFENSE AGAINST GUILT

What makes guilt so powerful and sometimes so confusing? The *Baker Encyclopedia of Psychology* says, "Guilt is one of the major emotions (anxiety being the other) that sets in motion the various psychological defense mechanisms." Defense mechanisms keep an individual from facing reality as it truly is.

As humans we often will do almost anything to avoid feeling guilt. Here are some of our psychological tricks:

1. Denial: "What, me? Responsible for the divorce? Sad about anything? Guilty of anything other than being a great husband/wife? You gotta be kidding! If you had to live with what I've had to live with, you'd be doing exactly what I have done."
2. Blaming others: "It's not my fault. It was the jerk I was married to."

3. Comparison with others: "I may have gotten divorced, but at least I didn't cheat on my husband/wife."
4. Overspiritualization: Some people become Bible-thumpers after divorce, quoting Scripture for every situation, and using Scripture as a weapon to point out the flaws in others, not least of whom is the ex-spouse. This use of Scripture is frequently an attempt to deny feelings of guilt. (It can also be a frightened attempt at creating some sense of order and stability in life.)
5. Overcompensation: "I may have failed in my marriage, but watch me fly now in my new (a) career, (b) dating relationships, (c) parenting role, (d) academic endeavor, (e) swinging lifestyle. . . ."
6. Repression/suppression: "Every time I think about it I feel so lousy, so I just don't think about it anymore."

Take a second look at this list, and you'll see that nearly all of these tacks are based in the first one—denial. In short, denial is a common precipitant of guilt and shame—denial of responsibility for failure, of pain, of sadness, fear, or anger, and so forth. Let's say a man is struggling with guilt feelings due to divorce. If he can deny any responsibility for the divorce, if he can deny that he's feeling like a failure, if he can deny his sad feelings about the impact of the divorce on the children, then he won't ache; he won't hurt. To accomplish this denial, he can resort to a host of defense mechanisms. As a matter of fact, almost anything can become such a defense.

Guilt and denial don't coexist well in the conscious mind. But guilt, even if denied and repressed, remains active within the body and can contribute to a long roster of maladies, such as migraine headaches, ulcers, back pain, high blood pressure, and heart attacks. The reason is simple: The body knows what goes on in the mind, even if the mind doesn't allow the rest of the world to see what's going on. The body responds to the turmoil of the mind.

THE MANY FACES OF GUILT

Some people believe that guilt is tied merely to societal standards; to handle guilt one need only come to terms with society's pressures—or reject society's values. But guilt's early formation and ongoing existence is not simply a matter of society's standards.

Bruce Narramore argues that guilt is a universal experience; we are not born morally neutral but have God's law written upon our hearts (see Rom. 2:14–15). This is one form of guilt. Let's look more closely at several types.

Objective Guilt

Objective guilt is a judicial term, representing a violation of law. The law broken may be a judicial or human law: A person is either driving within the legal speed limit or above it. To drive above the speed limit is to be objectively guilty of speeding. This guilt is a simple fact.

The second type of objective guilt has to do with a breach of God's law. For example, a divorcing person may be legally innocent of any breach of human law and yet be guilty of breaking God's law. God does write his will upon the scrolls of our hearts. As we breach his will, we are, at least until our consciences are dulled, internally reminded by the internal voice of conscience.

Subjective Guilt

The word *guilt* can also represent a subjective or emotional experience, as when one judges oneself to be in violation of a standard. One time several years ago I was driving down the road when a child ran out from behind a parked car, right into the side of my car. Fortunately the child just bounced off and was not injured. But suppose the child had been seriously injured or killed. I would have felt terrible—guilty—even though I had done nothing legally or morally wrong. At the very least I would have felt guilty for not driving defensively enough. Why didn't I see the legs and feet of a child between the parked cars?

It is possible to be objectively guilty and yet feel no subjective guilt. Take the sociopath who commits murder but feels no guilt. It is also (obviously) possible to feel subjective guilt when one is not objectively guilty of anything. This is sometimes called false guilt. Many who survived the Hiroshima blast felt guilty for surviving while family members died. Children caught in the presence of other children who are doing something wrong (stealing cookies, for instance) can feel guilty even though they did no wrong.

Subjective guilt can be constructive or destructive. *The Baker Encyclopedia of Psychology* explains that constructive sorrow ". . . focuses on the damage done to others, and the desire to make things right." Focused on future change, this guilt is based on and motivated by love. It uses the sorrow associated with guilt to make a constructive change so that one may make amends or at least avoid repeating the action that caused the guilt. This form of guilt is *other*-centered.

The second form of subjective guilt is self-centered and self-condemning. Sometimes called neurotic guilt, it focuses upon past failure and is based in anger, attempting to punish oneself (or others) enough to in some way make up for the act causing the guilt. Some neurotic patterns sound like this: "I was wrong. Stupid. Selfish. Irresponsible. I should have done better. I'll hate myself for the rest of my life. If I don't forgive myself and if I keep thinking bad things about myself, perhaps someday I will punish myself enough and the debt for my failure will be paid. I will in some way make amends for what I have done, or for what has happened in my life, by hating and punishing myself." People in this state of mind are frequently secretly wishing they could exert some control over the past.

Neurotic guilt can also be a dysfunctional attempt at regaining a relationship. The message sounds something like this: "If I can punish myself in such a mean and flagrant way that my ex-spouse can see I am really sorry for the situation, perhaps he or she will come back to me. If I can whip myself badly enough, perhaps my children will see my pain and stop being angry."

Neurotic guilt can lead to despair: "Nobody likes me. Everybody hates me. I might as well go out into the garden and eat some worms. Life will never be the same again. Everything's ruined, and I'm responsible." It also can lead to social isolation and fear: "I did such a poor job of my marriage that I think I'd better avoid anything in the future that looks challenging or risky."

This type of guilt is based on lies: Masochism says, "It feels good to feel pain." Distorted spirituality says, "You deserve to hurt." Broken dreams say, "You wasted your best opportunity." Childhood abandonment issues say, "You deserve to die." The messages aren't true and the lies need to be stared down.

This chart by Bruce Narramore summarizes the two forms of subjective guilt.[1]

	Psychological Guilt	Constructive Sorrow
Person in primary focus	Yourself	God or others
Attitudes or actions in primary focus	Past misdeeds	Damage done to others or our future correct deeds
Motivation for change (if any)	To avoid feeling bad (guilt feelings)	To help others, to promote our growth, or to do God's will (love feelings)
Attitude toward oneself	Anger & frustration	Love & respect, combined w/ concern
Result	(a) External change (for improper motivations) (b) Stagnation due to paralyzing effect of guilt (c) Further rebellion	Repentance and change based on an attitude of love and mutual respect

Guilt Versus Shame

Guilt and shame are frequently confused with each other. Simply stated, guilt is one's own reaction to one's own behavior; shame is one's response to others, as they observe one's behavior.

The word *shame* comes from Old English; it meant to cover or hide an exposure. Shame is usually a *reaction to* the negative evaluation of others. In *Fundamentals of Analysis*, F. Alexander indicated that guilt was a product of wrongdoing, while shame was born of feeling inferior. And H. M. Lynd (*On Shame and the Search for Identity*) felt that shame stemmed from some intimate, sensitive area of one's self being exposed to others.

Applied to the subject of divorce, subjective guilt is what you experience internally as a reaction to your own sense of right and wrong and your own inability to live up to your own standards. Shame, on the other hand, is what you experience internally as a reaction to what you believe others think about you. Shame is a breach in your ability to maintain your own personal pride as you relate to others about whom you care.

RESOLVING GUILT

Facing and resolving either guilt or shame is a difficult, challenging, and painful process, so painful that some will not want to walk through it.

Choose Health

The presence of illness sometimes reflects the desire for illness. It is not unusual for persons to remain ill by choice, since being ill satisfies or protects them in some way. They may wish to avoid responsibility. They may need others to reach out to them. Illness is frequently a choice. So also is healing.

The Bible tells of a man who had lain paralyzed for thirty-eight years. Thirty-eight long hot summers. Thirty-eight cold winters. When meeting the man the first question Christ asked was, "Do you want to get well?" (John 5:6). Stop reading for a moment and ask yourself: Do I want to be healed, and do I want to face the future rather than live in the past?

There is a cost either way. The costs of healing include personal change, maturation, and forgiveness of yourself and others. It is not easy to change or grow. But in change and growth, often, is also happiness, joy, freedom, and peace.

There is also a cost in not growing or healing. It is the cost of remaining controlled by the past, coupled with the almost certain probability that one will repeat it. In the end, it is always harder to change, grow, heal, and rebuild, but it is always better. And it is always a choice.

What is your choice?

Choose Honesty

Until you are willing to step squarely into the center of your real situation and accept the feelings and responsibilities of that situation, it is doubtful that you will be able to get beyond your guilt.

As painful as it may be, as much as it may lead temporarily toward depression, as much as it may elevate your anxiety, try to see your situation *as it really is*. No fantasy. No blaming. No denial of facts. Just as it really is.

If you were walking in the woods and came across a bear, would it really help the situation to pretend it wasn't there? Or to pretend it was a friendly kitten? Or to blame the National Park Service for allowing it to be there?

So it is with divorce. When we encounter personal failure, we tend to resist being completely honest with ourselves about our failure. We are more comfortable casting blame onto others, circumstances, our past, our upbringing, the failures of our parents, our spouse, our financial situation, our education, our body or face, our social circle, even God. We rationalize. We blame. We repress. We fight against accepting personal responsibility, and in doing so we become tied to our failures and the guilt and shame they drag behind them. We also become tied to the probability of making the same mistakes in the future.

It is important for you as a divorced person to be able to say, "I have made some mistakes. I carry some responsibility for the failure of my marriage. I feel like a failure. I hope my children will one day forgive me. I'm not very happy. This is where I am right now. The reality of my situation is not very pretty."

Until you fully recognize and accept the truth of your circumstances and your relationships you will not be able to move beyond them. The bear in the woods won't go away if you simply close your eyes. Your circumstances and relationships are potential mirrors to your inner self, if you allow them to be.

They do not create you; they can reflect to you a great deal about who you are.

As you accept your role in the problem, you can choose to change parts of the problem. If responsibility is denied, then the pattern leading up to the divorce is likely to be repeated. You cannot change how your ex reacted during marriage, but you can begin to assume full responsibility for your own future.

Analyze Your Guilt

The Action Items at the end of this chapter give specific questions to help you separate out your feelings of guilt from feelings of shame, your objective guilt from subjective guilt, your self-condemning, punitive guilt from healthy, constructive sorrow. If the very fact of your divorce (no matter what the circumstances) burdens you with what you identify as objective guilt—a sense that you have breached God's law—you might look ahead to chapter 10, "Biblical Perspectives on Divorce and Remarriage," for a closer look at the biblical teaching.

In your notebook lay out your situation—all the rational and irrational guilt you've been afraid to face.

Admit Your Powerlessness

The first step in any twelve-step program begins: "We admitted we are powerless. . . ." Stop for a moment and reflect upon your *own* powerlessness.

No matter what pieces of guilt and shame stare up at you from your notebook page, the best way to start resolving them is to admit that you are powerless against them. You can't fix it now. You can't relive or control the past. You can't make everyone happy again. You did what you could, and it wasn't enough. Stand for a moment stripped of your defenses and denials. "Yes, I am guilty and in that guilt I am powerless."

Go to God

The second and third of the twelve steps have to do with taking your guilt to God.

One of the greatest invitations anywhere is found in the Bible: "Come to me, all you who are weary and burdened, and I will give you rest" (Matt. 11:28). Yet as you read this, can you hear Shakespeare's Hamlet saying, "Ay, there's the rub!" That is, how does one go to God when one feels so separated from him and possibly so guilty in his presence?

It is important to understand that the feeling of separation from God is not only precipitated by divorce. C. S. Lewis in his book *A Grief Observed* struggled with the sense that God had abandoned him. He described how he came to God in his misery and found the doors of heaven bolted shut, nobody responding to his cries for help. He continued:

> Talk to me about the truth of religion and I'll listen gladly. Talk to me about the duty of religion and I'll listen submissively. But don't come talking to me about the consolation of religion or I shall suspect that you don't understand.

> If God's goodness is inconsistent with hurting us, then either God is not good or there is no God: for in the only life we know He hurts us beyond our worst fears and beyond all we can imagine.

Those are bitter words! Yet Lewis was not dealing with divorce. He was watching his wife slowly dies of cancer and struggling with an immense sense of separation from God. If Lewis sensed this spiritual gulf while living through the death of his wife, perhaps this sense of spiritual separation is not tied to guilt issues as much as to pain issues; pain can cloud the vision of God.

At moments of physical or relational pain so excruciating that I have wished I could pass out or even die, I have not been very accessible to loving relationships, no matter how freely the love was offered. I have been wrapped up in my own pain, unable to focus effectively or long upon anything else.

Refer again to page 75 and the meditation "Footprints." In the moments of our greatest pain when God may feel most distant, he is likely most active in moving us forward into the next stages of our lives. The point of all this: Don't believe that divorce is something that will cause God to hate or reject you. As you struggle with guilt and/or shame, take them *first* to God. Pray a lot. Even if the door to heaven seems slammed shut, it isn't. In his grief journey C. S. Lewis reached the point of writing:

> And so, perhaps, with God. I have gradually been coming to feel that the door is no longer shut and bolted. Was it my own frantic need that slammed it in my face? The time when there is nothing at all in your soul except a cry for help may be just the time when God can't give it: you are like the drowning man who can't be helped because he clutches and grabs. Perhaps your own reiterated cries deafen you to the voice you hoped to hear.

After admitting your powerlessness, go to God. Open your heart to him. Tell him exactly what you're experiencing. Open before him your notebook of guilt and shame. Ask for his grace, forgiveness, healing, and restoration.

First John 1:9 was written to Christians struggling with their own humanity: "If we confess our sins, he is faithful and just to forgive us our sins and purify us from all unrighteousness." His grace can cover your neurotic guilt as well as your objective guilt. Give it to God.

Be assured that Someone bigger than yourself can release you—indeed desires to release you, from your burden of guilt, anger, and pain. You must ask for this forgiveness, but having asked for it, you must also *accept* it.

Human pride frequently keeps us from accepting forgiveness. We hang onto guilt, saying to God, "I'm not quite done being bad or guilty yet. Leave me alone for a while." Do you want to be well? Give it to God.

Forgive Yourself

"How can I forgive myself when I recklessly dumped so much anger on my ex-spouse? How is it possible to recall all those bitter words? How can I forgive myself for hurting the children who will grow up essentially without one of their blood parents? How can I forgive myself for disappointing my parents?"

Even when you know you've been forgiven by God, it can be difficult to forgive yourself. Such forgiveness often comes gradually, and we will return to self-esteem issues in later chapters, but for now try this exercise: Look again at your notebook pages—the detailing of your guilt and shame. Place your hands over the pages and say, "For all of this, I forgive me." The past is in the past. You can't relive it.

Determine to do your best to grow and mature so you don't repeat old patterns. The next time old guilt condemns you, ask yourself how you can turn the feeling into a constructive rebuilding of your life.

Confess Your Part

It's been said that confession is good for the soul. It's also good for off-loading feelings of guilt and shame. "I made some mistakes. I was wrong. Please forgive." Yes it can seem humiliating, but the psychological rewards are great. Psalm 32:3–5 says:

> When I kept silent about my sin, my body wasted away
> Through my groaning all day long.
> For day and night Thy hand was heavy upon me;
> My vitality was drained away as with the
> fever-heat of summer.
> I acknowledged my sin to Thee,
> And my iniquity I did not hide;
> I said, "I will confess my transgressions to the Lord";
> And Thou didst forgive the guilt of my sin. (NASB)

To confess, you don't have to be able to fix anything. That is, if you're feeling guilty because of the impact of your divorce upon your kids, go to them and confess: "I can't fix our marriage, and I know it's hurting you kids a lot. I know that I'm partially responsible for the marriage not working. I want to tell you how sorry I am that you have to go through this. You are innocent victims of a terrible thing. Can you forgive me?" If a child says, "No, I can't," you have at least opened the door to future healing.

Confession may alleviate the shame you feel from certain people, especially family. "I feel as if I've disappointed you. I'm sorry that I have caused you this pain."

Perhaps confession will be easiest with your kids. Start with them. Then progress up the ladder of difficulty. Seek to complete this process with your ex-spouse—but after you've read the next chapter on forgiveness.

Forgiveness and Recompense

The next chapter deals with the issue of forgiving others. But here and now, as you work through your own guilt, understand at least for the moment that in offering forgiveness to your ex-spouse, in asking for forgiveness, and in doing whatever you can to make recompense for pain that you have caused, substantial pieces of the burden of guilt will be lifted.

Granted, you may never choose to remarry your ex-spouse. Yet constructive guilt says, "Learn to make peace. Learn to leave peace where there was once turmoil. Seek and offer healing. Use kindness rather than meanness; gentleness rather than harshness; compassion rather than slander; forgiveness rather than retaliation." That's how constructive guilt works.

Some pieces of guilt regarding your divorce may linger for a long time. There is no "magic wand" that quickly and easily makes it all go away. Some people try to use religion as a "magic wand" and when it doesn't work, some "lose their faith." Don't be disillusioned or feel hopeless if feelings of guilt or shame remain for a while. Use them as motivators to lead you to do what is right. Be patient and keep your feet walking down the road to wellness.

FAILURE IS NOT THE FINAL WORD

In *Divorce and the Gospel of Grace*, L. Woodson says, "Even though a divorce may be the best of all solutions to a hopelessly shattered relationship, there is still a sense of guilt. Divorce was just never meant to be. . . ." Divorce usually represents failure. Yet failure is not the final word—at least not for the Christian. Guilt and shame cannot become the grave of life for the person who learns to walk hand in hand with God. Woodson continues:

> Every day the Christian is enabled to begin again. He fails at many points, but at no time has he committed an unpardon-

able sin, as long as he keeps his faith in the power of Christ to save. There is no need for any man to exist under the weight of guilt when Christ forgives and accepts.

Guilt and shame are byproducts of failure, and divorce may be the greatest failure of a lifetime. Perhaps this is why Scripture has so much to say about hope! Failure is not the end of the story. There is freedom from guilt and shame. The very best source of that freedom is in walking close to God.

QUESTIONS FOR REFLECTION

1. Why do many people struggle with guilt or shame feelings in relation to their divorce?
2. Try to name at least five things about which you feel guilt or shame in regard to your divorce.
3. When you feel guilt or shame, do you tend to kick yourself? Kick others? Run away from facing them? Overcompensate? As you know yourself, what's your tendency?
4. In what way is unwillingness to forgive oneself an act of pride? How can a person hide behind failure to protect him- or herself against the challenge of growth?
5. If you had a magic wand, how would you use it in resolving feelings of guilt or shame? How would your wave of the wand affect those closest to you, as they deal with the divorce?
6. Why is confession listed as a mechanism for reducing guilt? What makes confession so difficult? To make any difference to whom does one go to confess?

ACTION ITEMS

Write one or more paragraphs in answer to each of the following questions:

1. In relationship to whom is your guilt or shame attached? Why?
   a. ex-spouse
   b. children
   c. parents, grandparents

d. friends

e. God, church, or religious community

f. self

g. other (who? why?)

2. Is the guilt you struggle with objective or subjective?

3. If objective, whose standards are being broken?

4. If subjective, are you using it constructively or destructively?

5. What's the difference between guilt and shame? Which are you experiencing in regard to whom? (Answer may be *both*; just be sure you know the difference.)

6. To learn to use subjective guilt constructively, write out a personal statement, a "manifesto," of how you will (intentionally and with purpose) use your guilt to make as positive a difference as possible, in all your relationships, but especially in those closest and/or most painful to you as you go through your divorce.

FOR SPIRITUAL GROWTH

1. Make a list of every divorce-related item about which you feel guilt or shame. Take the list to God in prayer. Where you need forgiveness, ask for it. Where there is no need to ask for forgiveness, pray for healing and restoration.

2. Read John 8:1–11 once more, putting yourself in the woman's place. Ask yourself how Christ would have handled you, with your faults and failures. Are you being harder on yourself than Christ would be if he were talking with you right now?

3. Do you think you have permission to fail? What do you believe God thinks about you when you fail? After answering those two questions, read the following Scriptures: John 13:36–38; John 18:15–27; John 21:1–19.

‡

CHAPTER 6

FACING FORGIVENESS

The heart knows its own bitterness.

Proverbs 14:10 (NASB)

There may be no more difficult challenge in working through the struggles of divorce than that of forgiveness. As one divorced person said, "Forget? Probably not. Forgive? Never!" How is it possible to forgive someone who hurt you so badly: someone who stuck the knife into your heart then twisted it again and again? Forgive the betrayal? The harsh words? The emotional vacuum with which you lived for those many years? The affair? The withdrawal of sexual intimacy? Forgive the meanness and the broken promises to love and cherish? The nasty court battles, the manipulation of the children, the lies? The self-centeredness? The agony of brokenness? Forgive? Never! To forgive would mean to let go of the anger, and sometimes the only control one seems to have in the midst of divorce is the right to one's anger. To forgive would mean to let go of the bitterness, and you may just not be ready yet to let go of it.

WHAT IS FORGIVENESS?

An old Webster's dictionary in my office defines the verb *forgive* as ". . . to cease to feel resentment against an offender;

to give up resentment of or claim to requital for an insult; to grant relief from payment of a debt.''

"To cease to feel . . .'' Is it possible to cease feeling the pain of a broken arm or a broken heart? No. It is not possible to cease to feel an emotion, including resentment against an offender. As discussed in earlier chapters, the best thing one can do with feelings is to accept them as they are felt. So this first segment of Webster's definition is not applicable as one wades through feelings about divorce.

"To give up resentment . . .'' This part of the definition implies that a decision may be made as to whether one will continue to use resentment as a means of punishment. The last part of the definition clarifies further: "to grant relief from payment of a debt.'' Hmm, forgiveness seems to be an act that has nothing to do with feelings.

This is the first lesson of forgiveness. It is a decision to grant pardon for a debt owed. Full pardon. No escape clauses. No exceptions.

Stop and reflect for a moment. Who "owes" you? Is your ex in debt to you? Your parents? Your kids? What interest is piling up as debts remain unpaid?

Allow me to propose another definition of *forgive* as it may specifically apply to divorce: to forgive is to be willing to give up one's rights to use one's legitimate club of anger as a tool to punish one's self or one's ex—both now and in the future. Forgiveness involves this acknowledgment: I will not use my anger to bash you or me anymore.

To forgive one's ex means (a) putting down the "club" of your legitimate anger; (b) being willing to never use it again; (c) coming out of the dark alley where you have been hiding in hopes of surprising your ex with a smashing blow to the teeth, the stomach, or the back of the head; and (d) never going back for the club or the dark alley.

To Forgive Doesn't Mean to Forget

Only God can intentionally forget. When he forgives, he remembers our sins no more (see Jer. 31:34). When we choose to forgive we still retain the memories of pain, anger, fear, and sadness that required forgiveness in the first place. Repression of these memories is not healthy. God gave us memory to help protect us from hurt. (There's a reason for remembering what it feels like to touch a hot stove.) Actually, forgiveness is a *decision one makes because one remembers.*

Forgiveness Doesn't Address the Cause of the Pain

If you kick me in the shins, I may choose to forgive you, but I can't be blamed if I step back from you for a while until I am sure you're not going to do it again. Forgiveness doesn't address the issue causing the pain. It only clears the air so that the issues can potentially be addressed in an atmosphere of minimal emotional pressure.

Forgiveness Doesn't Release One From Responsibility

If you kicked me in the shins, you're still responsible for your action, even after I forgive you. You are in no way released from the culpability of your act. In divorce, neither party is released from the culpability of his or her acts, even if forgiveness is liberally given all the way around.

Forgiveness Isn't a One-Time Act

Tomorrow, when I get out of bed and my shins still hurt, I may have to once again reconfirm my decision to forgive you. The pain may feel worse tomorrow than it does today. That's how pain is sometimes. I may have to forgive you several times, until the pain (and the anger) is gone.

In Matthew 18, Peter asked Christ, "How many times do I have to forgive someone? Seven times?" Seven times may seem a lot on paper . . . unless you've been married longer than two weeks.

Christ responded, "Not seven times, but seventy-times-seven times." Unless I flunked third-grade math, that's 490 times. There are at least two thoughts worth considering here. First, forgiveness isn't something one does just once and then it's done. The deeper the pain, the more times you may have to release it and let it go before it truly leaves. It may take more than 490 times. Christ wasn't placing a limit on forgiveness. He was teaching that real forgiveness may take hundreds of times to accomplish.

The second point may be more profound: If Scripture teaches us to forgive 490 times, how many times do you think God may be willing to forgive you? Your ex? The other people who have caused you pain?

THE BENEFITS OF FORGIVENESS

Unforgiveness usually ends up doing far more damage to the person doing the *un*forgiving than it ever does to the person being *un*forgiven. Forgiveness is not so much for the other person's benefit as for your own. Here are a few positive principles of forgiveness:

Forgiveness Frees You From the Ownership of the Past

After divorce some people spend a great deal of emotional energy scheming about ways to get even. Some use friends or relatives to "kick" the ex-spouse. Some use anonymous phone calls to employers. Some use the court system. Some put sand in gas tanks or plant marijuana in the ex-spouse's backyard and then call the police. (It's true.) Others, too timid to take any overt action, spend months, even years, fantasizing about retribution. Still others become involved in ongoing court battles.

All of this does one thing very effectively: It keeps you involved with your ex, and it keeps you tied up in the ongoing pain of the divorce. The more energy one gives to getting even, venting anger or sadness, the more one is *owned* by the divorce. To forgive is to provide a means of moving away from the pain.

Forgiveness Breaks the Cycle of Retribution

Divorce doesn't happen because both spouses are wildly in love with each other and happy with the marriage. It happens because something was out of whack on both sides of the relationship and those broken pieces began hurting the marriage, much like a loose spoke on a bicycle wheel will hurt a rider as it whips the leg on every revolution.

When relational pain and accompanying anger last long enough, people start lashing out at each other, sometimes overtly with fists or words; sometimes covertly with affairs, emotional distance, and passive aggression.

As spouses lash out, the marital war escalates. Bill calls Sue a jerk. Sue calls Bill a horse's rear end. Bill throws a book at Sue. Sue leaves the room, slamming the door, and then throws Bill's favorite sneakers into the trash. Bill finds out and then delays getting Sue's car repaired. Sue escalates by burning supper or by getting home so late she can't fix supper at all. Bill sleeps in another room. Sue calls an old boyfriend and starts an emotional affair. Bill stays at work until ten every night, and Sue tells the kids that Dad's having emotional problems.

The spiral can end in divorce, and after physical separation, the spiral can escalate rapidly, even dangerously. Bill moves out but needs the socks he left behind. When he comes home Sue has changed the locks. He quits paying the bills. Sue hires an attorney to make him pay the bills. Bill cleans out the retirement savings and squirrels the money away in a hidden account. Sue gouges the paint in Bill's new car with a key or a knife and the next morning finds her tires slashed. Bill comes home to get his golf clubs. Sue won't let him in the door, so he breaks in, punches Sue in the stomach, and tells her the worst is yet to come if she doesn't back down. Sue files for a restraining order from a judge. Up and up it spirals.

The cycle doesn't stop just because a judge drops his gavel and declares a marriage has ended. In fact, sometimes the cycle takes new and even more dangerous upward jags after divorce. The movie *The War of the Roses* portrays a gruesome end: One spouse being willing to die if it means the death of the other.

At some point, at least one of the two spouses must decide to stop the escalation, to be the more mature of the two, to forgive and seek peace.

Question: How high must the stakes get before there is irreparable damage? How grisly must the battle get before the children are scarred for life? How much hatred and bitterness are you willing to allow to become part of you, part of your personality, your soul? There is a saying worth noting: If you choose to get into a spraying contest with a skunk, even if you win, you come away smelling bad. So it is with the cycle of retribution or vengeance.

Several times the Scriptures say that vengeance is God's responsibility, not ours (see Rom. 12:19, for instance). Let God do what he decides should be done—in his good time. For the time being, for your own mental health, choose to forgive.

Forgiveness Facilitates Personal Healing and Growth

How can my healing begin when I am still wielding the knife of my own bitterness, causing wounds in others but in the process also continuing to cause my own blood to run?

Scripture gives powerful but difficult advice in this regard: "Love your enemies, and pray for those who persecute you" (Matt. 5:44). God didn't give this instruction so our enemies could feel the sting of our self-righteousness but so we could learn how to get rid of the anger that otherwise would destroy— guess who?—us! It's true, one can't very well hate someone and at the same time ask God to heal and bless that person. The two don't fit well together. The question to ask yourself is to what depth do you wish to heal?

Decide to stop using your anger to punish your ex, and you are ready to concentrate on your own healing. It takes emotional and spiritual energy to hang on to anger and pain. Just try to imagine the possibilities of rechanneling that energy.

Forgiveness can be an effective pressure valve, allowing a person to move past the crippling logjam of emotions.

Through Forgiveness You Can Gain Personal Dignity

Often just the reverse is believed. Many people act as if personal dignity is best protected by being the one who hits the hardest. But there comes a point at which further escalation is nothing but further absurdity, where the only end product is being smeared further with the feces of hatred and bitterness. This is human dignity?

Many warring spouses or ex-spouses begin to look like each other, wearing the same clothing of wrath and poison. This is human dignity?

How much better to control the outcome of one's situation by choosing to forgive. One usually cannot exert much real control over the separated or ex-spouse. If that fact were not apparent before separation, it rapidly becomes crystal clear after separation, and doubly clear after divorce.

One can, on the other hand, control one's own destiny, freeing oneself from those smothering webs of bitterness (and its cohorts—ulcers, colitis, high blood pressure, frowny faces, migraine headaches) by choosing to forgive. There is immense control and incalculable strength in the simple statement, "You cannot hurt me anymore. I have moved beyond your anger and bitterness, because I forgive you."

FORGIVING YOUR EX

There's nothing fun about forgiving someone who's hurt you. But as distasteful as it may be, it's still in your best interest to forgive your ex. In her book *A Stone for a Pillow*, Madeleine L'Engle has a chapter titled "Bless the Bastard." That feeling is not far off the mark, as one considers releasing ownership of a legitimate grudge. Incidentally, the concept of blessing (or forgiving) the bastard has a biblical base, found in Romans 5:8: "While we were still sinners, Christ died for us." In his grace, God reaches out to forgive us.

A factor in this process may cause you deep distress: In forgiveness there is also the possibility of reconciliation.

Forgiveness may or may not lead to remarrying one's ex-spouse, but it should lead to a cessation of hostilities and at least open the door to mutual repentance and reconciliation.

One of the most poignant stories coming out of the Vietnam War involved an American soldier who had killed a North Vietnam Army regular in battle. After the firefight was over, the soldier went to the body of the dead enemy soldier and took out the man's wallet. In the wallet was a picture of the man's family and an address.

After the American soldier returned home, he wrote a short

letter to the Vietnamese soldier's parents. He said that he was sorry for killing their son. He had been drafted. He had not chosen to go to war, but in the moment of battle, he had acted on instinct. He then said, "I beg your forgiveness."

Months passed. One day he received an envelope with a Vietnamese stamp. It was a letter from the dead soldier's parents. It contained a simple, profound sentence: "We forgive you. Will you now be our son?"

Forgiveness opens the door to healing, no matter how deep the wound. It also opens the door to the potential of reconciliation. It is one of the most difficult, but one of the most healing, things you can do.

There are several steps to forgiving someone else—including your ex-spouse. At first the attempt to forgive may be faltering, like a baby learning to walk. It's okay. Remember, all babies have to learn to walk before they can run.

Be Honest About the Problem

Divorce usually doesn't happen in a vacuum. There are always two people involved in it, and each person bears his or her own part of the responsibility for the divorce. Always.

In the previous chapter you took an honest look at your own responsibility. As you get a clearer focus of your own faults, reevaluate the blame you place on your ex-spouse. Focus your sight on truth; self-recrimination or blaming, magnifying or minimizing either personal responsibility or the ex-spouse's responsibility, extended pity-trips or spouse-bashing—none of these are centered in the truth. (Don't worry about whether your ex is being completely honest. That's between your ex and God.)

Allow God to Forgive

Try to grab hold of the truth that God offers his forgiveness to your ex-spouse, just as God offers it to you. God is not wrapped up in the issue of who's to blame. His concern is not so much his anger about divorce, as it is his sadness at the suffering of those whom he loves and their concern as to whether he will be allowed to help extricate both parties from their web of hurt, sadness, fear, anger, revenge, blame, and anxiety. The question from our human perspective is whether we are willing to accept what God has to offer, and his forgiving grace floods our spirits as we choose to forgive others.

Let Go

Letting go means a lot of things. Letting go of the past. Letting go of fantasies of retribution. Letting go of anger, sadness, fear. Letting go of dreams, now shattered. Letting go of control. Letting go of your need for answers. You may never know why your ex-spouse did what he or she did. This may be the point at which you can stop asking why. (If you knew the reason behind every painful situation, would it really hurt any less? It might hurt more!)

There's a little saying that many people use during this process of forgiveness: "Let go and let God." The more one attempts to control the past via refusing to forgive, the less one is in control of one's own future. To allow God to handle unfinished business also allows God the freedom to guide and direct one's future.

Remember that forgiveness is not a one-time event. It's an act of the will, to be repeated like good medicine as often as needed, until the anger, pain, sadness, and fear are completely gone.

Don't worry about feelings. They're like a caboose following a locomotive: They eventually follow actions. Choose to forgive. It may take time, but eventually your feelings will mirror your decisions. Trust the process of forgiveness.

Ask for and Offer Forgiveness

Jesus said, "If you hold anything against anyone, forgive him, so that your Father in heaven may forgive you your sins" (Mark 11:25).

And in another context: "Go and be reconciled to your brother; then come and offer your gift [at the altar]" (Matt. 5:24).

In the previous chapter we addressed the issue of asking for forgiveness, especially from children and parents. It may be easiest to seek forgiveness from your ex-spouse as you *offer* it.

To whom does one offer forgiveness? Start with the ex-spouse. After that, everything else in life will be easy. A funny saying may be appropriate at this point: "If you have to swallow a number of frogs, start with the biggest one." In this case, the "biggest one" will probably be your ex-spouse. Go to your ex and admit your faults and flaws. Ask for forgiveness and offer it too, even if your ex doesn't ask for forgiveness.

To grow through divorce you may need to look back over your life and forgive your parents. There is frequently a correlation between people who have been divorced and people who have been hurt by their parents. It makes sense, actually. If Mother emotionally abandoned her infant son, and he then marries (and later divorces) a controlling woman (in a subconscious attempt to make up for the loss of Mom), is his anger toward his wife or mother?

If Dad was "too busy" for his daughter, who grew up with an emotional vacuum, and she married and divorced a husband who was also too busy for her, whom does she resent? Husband or Daddy?

Divorce, then, is frequently an event set into motion by influences from past years. To heal from divorce you may need to sort out the original pain and choose to forgive other parties.

Make Recompense Where Possible

Seeking and giving forgiveness is the most difficult step for most people in divorce recovery.

As you ask for and give forgiveness, take a final step and ask if there is any way you can make recompense.

Oh, sure! She'll ask for triple the child support the court ordered, or he'll ask for full custody of the kids. Well, that's not exactly what recompense is about. Those examples have more to do with extending the battle than in seeking to make recompense for past pain.

To make recompense, men should be on time with child support checks, could offer to fix a leak or a flat tire, and should be kind in all aspects of the relationship. Women can be flexible with visitation rights and kind in all their communication. Both men and women should seek peace, be gentle, and look for ways to relieve tension or ease pain.

How you make recompense will depend upon the specifics of your relationship with your ex. You may want to write a long letter, do it on the phone, or do it in person.

Here's how it should sound when it happens. Whether you choose to use these exact words is not important:

> I know I have hurt you. I'm sorry. I have been responsible for much of the pain and problems we have had. I accept responsibility for my part in this divorce, and for wounding you (and the children, if there are any).
>
> The reason I'm (here, calling, or writing) is that I want to ask for your forgiveness. You might not want to give it. If that's the case, I'll understand, but at least I need to ask for it.
>
> I also want to ask if there are ways I can mend any fences, make any recompense, or help ease any tensions I have created. I may not have the guts to do it, but I want to know if there's any way I can make up for some of the pain I have caused in this divorce.

There may be requests with which you cannot comply, and you are always free to say no if asked to go beyond safe or appropriate boundaries. A sexually or physically abusive husband may request that his ex-wife remarry him as an act of recompense. An enraged wife may ask that her ex-husband kill himself as an act of recompense. Most often no specific thing will be requested. The fact that you have offered to make recompense will speak for itself.

On the other hand, there may be some ways in which you may be able to take some small action to help a difficult situation. At the very least, you will be lifting part of a large, painful, and long-lasting load from the shoulders of at least two people in the world: your ex-spouse and yourself.

You may hear your ex-spouse choking on the other end of the phone line.

Deep fear or sadness may surface and your ex may cry or

withdraw from you in confusion. Respond by accepting the feelings expressed and asking for forgiveness.

But things may not go so smoothly. In fact, your ex may respond with a rush of anger, venting his or her feelings. If this happens, your response, again, can be simple: Accept the feelings expressed and apologize for your part in creating them. Once those feelings have been poured out, perhaps even more than once, the relationship can begin to heal and your future contacts with each other will be less painful. This will be particularly important if you have children, if there are ongoing financial involvements, or if the two of you live in the same city.

FREE INDEED

Whether your ex-spouse asks for forgiveness or offers to make recompense is not important if you have truly forgiven, as giving forgiveness is not dependent on receiving it in return. Your ex-spouse may or may not forgive you. His or her response is not your problem. The challenge of this step is not upon your ex-spouse's shoulders. Even if he or she tells you where you can stuff your request for forgiveness, you have at least accomplished one necessary item in your own road to personal restoration: To the best of your ability, you have cleared the air. You may now, in all good conscience, walk away from the power struggles you've had with each other. You are free to move on. Your ex-spouse's anger, fear, and sadness are completely his or hers, not yours.

Seeking forgiveness, offering it if asked for, and attempting to make recompense may stretch your credibility with your ex-spouse. He or she may not believe you are serious! He or she may suspect that you are attempting to manipulate the situation for your own gain, and in a small way, you are. You are working hard at cleaning your own slate so you may move forward with the growth and challenge that lies ahead of you. You are trying to reduce the pain of the divorce for all parties concerned.

Remember, once you've swallowed the biggest frog, the smaller ones will be much easier.

QUESTIONS FOR REFLECTION

1. As you wade through the issues of your divorce, do you tend to take on much of the responsibility for it, or do you dump most of the responsibility onto your ex-spouse? Are you dealing with the truth and honesty?
2. In one sentence describe the greatest hurdle you will face in the process of forgiving your ex-spouse.
3. How do blame, self-pity, self-recrimination, and spouse-bashing all end up tying one to the ongoing pain of divorce?
4. In your notebook write your own definition of forgiveness. "To me, forgiveness means . . ."
5. Write your own definition of recompense. "To me, recompense means . . ."
6. Is it harder for you to forgive your ex-spouse or yourself? Why?
7. Try to identify two things you need to forgive your parents for.

ACTION ITEMS

1. Begin each day for one month with a short prayer asking God to help you forgive yourself and those who have hurt you.
2. If you need to work up to the tasks of forgiving your ex and making some attempt at recompense, circle a date on your calendar at which you will begin this process. On that date:
   a. contact your ex (in person, by phone, or by letter), and ask for forgiveness;
   b. take some small step at making recompense.
3. Forgiveness, much like a pair of scissors, has two blades and one will not work without the other. The first blade is that of giving forgiveness. The other blade is that of receiving forgiveness. Write a two-page statement describing the potential impact of your giving and receiving forgiveness. Refer to the following individuals:

a. yourself (including impact on your self-respect/self-esteem);
b. your children if there are any, and their relationships with both you and your ex;
c. your ex;
d. your parents (if they're alive).

FOR SPIRITUAL GROWTH

1. Review the following scriptural verses having to do with forgiveness; reflect on them as they apply to your situation:

   "If your brother [or husband or wife] offends you, take him to task about it [don't ignore, deny, or repress it], and if he is sorry forgive him. Yes, if he wrongs you seven times in one day and turns to you and says, I am 'sorry' seven times, you must forgive him." And the apostles said to the Lord, "Give us more faith" (Luke 17:3–5 PHILLIPS).

   "Forgive us our debts [sins, trespasses, wrongdoings], as we [in the same way that we, at the same level that we] also have forgiven our debtors [those who have wronged us]" (Matt. 6:12).

   "For if you forgive other people their failures, your Heavenly Father will also forgive you. But if you will not forgive other people, neither will your Heavenly Father forgive you your failures" (Matt. 6:14–15 PHILLIPS).

   "And whenever you stand praying, you must forgive anything that you are holding against anyone else, and your Heavenly Father will forgive you your sins [failures, in the Greek]" (Mark 11:25 PHILLIPS).

2. Read Psalm 109 and consider whether David had problems with forgiveness.

3. Read Proverbs 19:11; 24:17; 25:21. Reflect on these texts as they apply to your situation.

4. Read Matthew 5:7. Reflect on this text as it applies to your situation.

✝

CHAPTER 7

CHILDREN OF DIVORCE

Perhaps the most difficult thing, for me at least, was dealing with the children. Their pain hurt me far more than anything else I can think of. It still hurts me to think about it. Perhaps it always will.

If there are children within the divorcing family system, this chapter may be one of the most vital in the book. All children, of all ages, are affected by divorce.

For the children, divorce represents a "ripping apart" of relationships that are at least as powerful and traumatic as that faced by the divorcing spouses—and often more so. It represents the destruction of the child's home, and this wreaks havoc on the child's self-identity and self-esteem. Even within severely dysfunctional families, divorce is usually seen by children as an enemy. Except in the most unusual circumstances, children are deeply hurt and angered when their parents choose to divorce.

Consequently, both spouses need to learn how to communicate with the children—no matter what age the children are. When faced with any major trauma, human beings in general and children in particular need to make as much sense as possible out of chaos. They need to understand, organize, interpret, and regain some semblance of order in a life that has become frighteningly disorganized and out of control.

HOW TO TELL YOUR CHILD ABOUT YOUR DIVORCE DECISION

Though there is no simple formula for this process, here are some thoughts that may be helpful.

1. Gear the information to fit the child's age and ability. A four-year-old probably won't understand about adultery or mental cruelty, but a twelve-year-old probably will.
2. Be honest and open, but speak the truth tempered by love. Remember, the children's self-esteem and self-identity is tied to both you and your ex. Engaging in spouse-bashing in the presence or hearing of your kids will damage your kids, and in the end will possibly alienate them from you.
3. If possible, both Mother and Father should be present when explaining why the divorce is happening. If both parents' presence is impossible, then both parents should separately take the time to explain, from their perspective, why they're getting divorced.
4. If the issue of responsibility must be addressed (that is, if the kids are asking who's at fault):
   a. Be sure to explain that the children are *not* at fault.
   b. Be sure to explain that both Mom and Dad bear responsibility, if not equally, at least mutually.
5. Express your own feelings, but carefully. Your children need to understand your feelings, but your expression of the depth of your pain could overwhelm them. Be careful not to crush your child with the weight of your own feelings. Your child has enough feelings to handle without having to carry or sort through yours as well.
6. Answer any questions they ask, but don't overload them with information you think they need. If you load them down with your feelings, they may suspect you're trying to manipulate them.

7. If you are able, pray with them. Take everything—every concern, every feeling—to God, holding hands as a family as you pray together. The kids will need to feel and experience some sense of family belonging, and prayer is a powerful avenue for meeting this need. Besides, the Lord is able to heal in circumstances beyond our wildest hope of resolution. If you can't pray with your kids, let them see you on your knees praying. Lead by doing.

IT'S HARD TO DEAL WITH ALL THE FEELINGS I'M HAVING

Name any emotion you've had in your divorce, and it's likely that your child has had the same feeling, perhaps at a greater intensity. Many parents fail to recognize that their children are experiencing immense and chaotic emotions because of the divorce. The pain of losing a parent through divorce can be worse than that of losing a spouse through divorce.

Adults frequently fail to recognize the relationship between the divorce and their child's altered behavioral patterns. Children often express their feelings by acting them out, and the younger the child the more this is true: throwing a toy to express anger; kicking the dog or a brother or sister to express frustration; running away to express fear; crying uncontrollably to express sadness; becoming a problem at school to express chaos and suffering. Some children become perfectionists, bringing home all A's, trying to maintain a sense of control. Some withdraw into depression; some mask depression by becoming exceptionally gregarious.

When going through divorce, children's behaviors can change, sometimes dramatically. The younger the child, the more the child will tend to "act out" his or her feelings. When this occurs, pay attention. Divorcing parents frequently make the mistake of interpreting the child's behavior as just one more problem with which the adult has to reckon—rather than seeing it as a signal of the child's pain. Learn to "read" your children's actions so you can "hear" their feelings.

Here are a few tips for helping your children deal with their feelings:

1. Encourage your children to express their own feelings, but don't demand that they do so. They will when they are ready, and they may not be ready for a long time. But *always* be ready to listen. The younger the child, the less able he or she will be to express feelings.
2. Especially if you are the custodial parent and/or the mother, expect your children to aim their anger at you. The noncustodial parent may not receive the level of real communication that is "enjoyed" by the custodial parent. Much of that real communication can be desperately angry, far more angry than the child may even know. As you work through the divorce and its issues with your children, expect them to lash out. Moms usually get kicked more than dads do. Though much of their anger is with the situation, it is unfortunately directed at you as a person.
3. Encourage them to *identify* what they're feeling. (Is it anger, sadness, fear? About what are they angry, sad, or fearful?)
4. Learn to accept and express your own feelings as they occur, and encourage your children to do the same. (A toothache doesn't go away just because someone says it shouldn't be there; neither does anger, sadness, or fear.)
5. *Accept* your children's feelings as expressed—even if this is uncomfortable for you. Don't argue, moralize, deny, or use any other form of shutting down their sharing of their feelings. Just listen and be thankful they have the courage to trust you with their real feelings.
6. Review the stages in the grief cycle and look for these stages in your children's lives, acted out at their individual levels of maturity.
7. Consider finding a support group specializing in helping children of divorcing families. It might help a child to be in touch with another child who has been through divorce and is two or three years away from the experience. Children can share common experiences

and be supportive in a way that adults and children cannot. Churches sometimes have programs for children of divorce.

Your child may go through a period of wondering if he or she will ever be happy again. Recent research is concluding that there may be no end to the pain experienced by children as their parents divorce. To a greater or lesser degree, the kids will hurt for the rest of their lives because of the divorce. That's the bad news.

The good news is that with the passage of time the pain will slowly begin to subside, and what may today be a sharp throb will someday become a dull ache. As rough as that is to accept, it's better to deal with the truth than to tell the kids that someday they'll magically understand and will accept the divorce.

HOW COULD GOD HAVE ALLOWED THIS TO HAPPEN?

Adults aren't the only ones who ask profound questions when they hurt. Kids often pass through a "faith crisis" as they watch their parents split apart. Frequently, children pray for, fantasize, and talk about their parents' reunion. (Sometimes they even attempt, in their own childlike ways, to engineer such reunions. If you want to understand the desire of most kids going through divorce, rent the Disney movie *The Parent Trap*.) If the parents don't rejoin in marriage, the children's faith is often at risk: "God didn't hear me." "God doesn't love me." "There is no God." "I'm too bad a person for God to care about."

Another faith issue is sometimes even more destructive in the lives of children in divorcing church families. Especially if Mom or Dad has been involved in some aspect of church leadership, service, or ministry, the children have probably learned that divorce is not God's wish. As these kids watch their parents divorce, they begin to question their parents' faith (or commitment to it) in very personal terms: "This faith isn't for me; it sure didn't do much for you."

Children above the age of eight or so often are disillusioned and angry toward authority, including God. "How could God let this happen? Why doesn't he stop it? Why doesn't he just make Mom and Dad get along with each other? What's wrong with him?''

Some children are sophisticated enough to verbalize the question: "If God is all-powerful and all-loving, why doesn't he intervene and stop this?'' Other children may simply feel that God doesn't exist or that he lied to them. Some may feel he doesn't care.

In helping children deal with these faith issues, consider these two thoughts and explanations. First, God allows us the freedom to do what we choose. God doesn't stop a child from stealing a cookie. He doesn't stop a vandal from throwing a rock through a window. And he doesn't stop mothers and fathers from divorcing. He chooses to let us make our own decisions, even if they hurt us or others.

Second, with every choice comes consequences. Cookie thieves sometimes ruin their suppers, and, when caught, sometimes get their hands slapped. Vandals sometimes end up at police stations. And divorce causes its own special kind of pain. Pain is a usual consequence of divorce.

Help your children understand that while God allows us to hurt ourselves and each other, he also has provided us with salve to rub on our wounds. God has promised, for example, to be a father to the fatherless (see Ps. 10:14; 68:5; 146:9). We are promised God's attention and support, especially in times of pain (see Jer. 30:17; Mal. 4:2; Matt. 11:28–30; 1 Pet. 5:7). While he was on earth, Christ demonstrated a real love for children (see Matt. 19:14; Mark 10:14; Luke 18:16), and we may be certain that his concern for children has not changed, since God doesn't change.

One of the great services any parent can offer a child, particularly in times of deep pain such as divorce, is that of showing the child how to take one's pain to the Lord and invite him into the healing process. Even the youngest child can open his or her heart to the healing hand of the Almighty. Parents can help in this process by leading the way.

YOUR CHILDREN AND YOUR EX-SPOUSE

One of the greatest dilemmas of a child in a divorcing family is feeling caught in a war and having to choose sides. A battle for the child's affections and allegiance simply damages the child.

There are many techniques by which parents attempt to manipulate their children toward themselves and away from the other parent. Some parents tell every grisly detail and exaggerate to drive home points. One scenario is the rag-doll syndrome. One parent uses the child to hit the other parent as if the child were a rag doll. But the harder the hit, the more destructive it is to the rag doll, and in the end the rag doll falls apart. Others give excessive gifts (the Santa Clause syndrome) to draw the child. Some make up stories; others use truth as a club. Some use depression, deep sighing, or tears to tear at the child's heart.

One of these manipulative battlegrounds involves visitation and time—who gets how much?

You may secretly wish that your ex lived on the moon, but unless there is overt sexual, physical, or other highly damaging abuse (in those cases it may be necessary to obtain a court order keeping the damaging parent from contact with the child), your children need ongoing contact with both parents. Here are a few reasons:

1. Your children's self-identity is tied to *both* parents.
2. Your children need some contact with your ex for them to make *their own* evaluations of him or her as a parent and to sort out *their own* answers about the reasons for the divorce.
3. Your ex will probably continue to be a source of role modeling for your children.
4. Younger children sometimes don't distinguish between Mom and Dad, but look at both parents as a unit. Visitation can help restore some sanity to a younger child's life.
5. Children need to know and feel that although their parents are divorced, both Mother and Father still love them.

6. Children's emotional healing following divorce usually occurs more effectively and smoothly when there is contact with both parents.
7. The children deserve time with both parents. They've been hurt and lost a lot, too.

It is not uncommon for parting spouses to assume that their children's ongoing relationship with their ex-spouse would be harmful to the kids. Some parents go as far as making public or legal accusations against their ex-spouse—to keep the children away from him or her. If you have this concern, you might seek the opinions of a few *neutral* individuals (clergy, social worker, therapist, or network of friends) who know both you and your ex-spouse. Avoid escalating the situation by allowing your anger and desire for revenge to play itself out in manipulative games with your ex, using your children's lives and emotions as pawns. Keep the best interests of your *children*, their needs and rights, at the forefront of your thoughts.

If you can't think beyond your own needs, consider these reasons why an ongoing relationship between your kids and your ex-spouse may be beneficial to you.

1. Your children may resent *you* later in life if they feel you have sabotaged their relationship with their other parent. Sooner or later they *will* mature to adulthood; they *will* learn the truth. More than likely they will also learn to "read" any manipulation that occurred and will then respond to it. You don't want to lose their love later by forcing them to choose you now.
2. If your ex is paying child support, time together with the children will encourage emotional involvement with and attachment to them. This, in turn, encourages timely payment of child support.
3. Think of your freedom and sanity: Visitation can give you time away from the demands of parenting. The lack of "time off" is often one of the biggest problems seen in single parenting.
4. If problems arise with your child, corrective action, whether it be discipline or simple correction of the

child's attitudes or behaviors, will be easier if you have the ongoing and united input of both parents.

As you establish the attitude you will have toward the relationship between your children and your ex, consider these additional thoughts:

1. You'll feel less resentful if you work at developing an attitude of cooperation. You might even try to give your ex a pat on the back for his or her involvement with the kids.
2. Work at making the visitation time pleasant for your children and for your ex, or you may incur the wrath of both. (Have the kids ready on time, with clean clothes, bags packed if needed, back home on time. Be pleasant for the children's sake.)
3. Encourage communication between your children and ex-spouse. If your ex is really as bad as you feel, your kids will eventually see it, too.
4. Choose a time for visitation that is good for all parties. In other words, avoid intentionally choosing times that you know will be difficult for your ex-spouse.
5. Make pick-ups and drop-offs as emotionally easy as possible for all parties: your kids, your ex, and you.
6. Think positive, be positive. Remember, it's not your ex but your children who will end up paying for your bad behavior or attitudes.
7. Plan something for yourself to enjoy during your free time. Get away from the house. Go to a movie with a friend. Go window shopping. Go for a bicycle ride or a walk in a park. Have a picnic for yourself. Be nice to you.

Your kids may not share your opinion regarding your ex. In fact, they probably won't. They probably still love your ex, even if there was a dysfunctional and damaging relationship between parent and children. One can divorce a mate but not a parent.

There is an even larger issue at stake. Your children will learn how to play the same games they see you playing. They will take your games into their own relationships. Eventually they'll use your tactics against you. The ultimate question is how will your children conduct and view *themselves* based on what they learn from your attitudes and behavior with your ex-spouse and with them?

Don't make the children pick sides. To try to unduly affect their decisions will hurt them, and will, later on, likely result in their anger against the manipulative parent. Nobody appreciates having been manipulated.

WHAT KIND OF A FAMILY ARE WE GOING TO HAVE NOW?

Younger children involved in divorce live in fear that the custodial parent will leave also. This fear, combined with the normal destruction of the child's sense of family, creates a heightened sense of loss and terror.

Certainly the family is going to be different after divorce. Certainly the children are going to have their own struggles as they learn to cope without the close interaction of one parent. This does not mean, however, that a single-parent family cannot be successful, close, and functional. In reality, some families become closer after divorce than they were prior to it. Sometimes divorce can create a stronger sense of family.

Being a single parent, especially with younger children, is an immense challenge. From where do you draw the needed additional energy to make a successful family? This is especially challenging within the first year of divorce, in the face of what are often numbing emotions, financial stress, possible relocation, overwhelming responsibilities, coupled with a strong desire to withdraw from the pressure and pain.

Creating belonging, support, mutual affirmation, caring, respect, mutual responsibility, and in general creating a positive family system after divorce may be challenging, but the principle is true: What you decide to happen will eventually happen if you have sufficient resolve to *make* it happen. The single parent has a choice as to what he or she will do about providing a sense of family for the children. That choice may involve changing one's priorities.

There are advantages in being a single parent, one of which is having greater control over what the family experience and identity will be. Leadership is not shared with another person. One can set a more clear path toward one's objectives. In this regard, here are a few tips:

1. Read. This is a new ball game; learn the new rules. There are many books on the subject. You don't have to do this in a vacuum.
2. Find other single parents. Talk with other single parents. You'll probably get a lot of support and answers from them.
3. Create regular family times and traditions. Set apart an evening or two each week strictly for family purposes (discussion, games, an outing, watching a favorite movie, going for walks, having gripe sessions, talking about school or job experiences). Create new family "traditions," which can provide a sense of family identity. They can be as lighthearted as building a family snowman at the first snow fall of every winter or as serious as praying together every evening.
4. Create family standards. In any family it is important to clearly communicate the rules, standards, and expectations, as well as to build toward common values and dreams. Help the children to understand that "this family stands for certain things, and this is one of them." Make them positive things. A person's life-long values come primarily from families during the first years of life. Give your kids a family identity. Don't feel so badly for the kids that you abandon all family standards in an attempt to make it up to the child.
5. Provide the children with healthy role models. When you see good characteristics in people, things you wish your children to model, point them out. Use friends, family members, neighbors, or people from church to provide multiple examples to your children regarding what you would hope they might be like when they grow up. Point out both successful and unsuccessful models so the children can observe and compare.

6. Establish household responsibilities and routines. Help the kids see that you all have to pull together even more now than before. Give chunks of responsibility to the children, geared of course to their abilities and levels of maturity.

7. Take family vacations. It doesn't have to be Disney World. Minivacations can be fun. Weekend trips to a local state park or camping in the rough with a borrowed tent don't cost much and can be lots of fun. If you plan the vacation together, it'll be even better.

8. If you date, talk with the kids about your dating. You may find that the kids see anyone you date as an intruder. On the other hand, they may see your date as a replacement for their lost parent. They may expect that you will not date at all. Regardless of *what* you do about dating, your kids will almost certainly have their own agenda and/or expectations for your dating partners. Talk about this—whom you date and what you did on your dates. Talk about what you think and feel about those you date. Ask your kids what they think and feel about those whom you date. Assure your kids that you won't take any steps toward marriage without speaking with them about it. Until you remarry, your first priority has to be the welfare and support of your children.

Avoid putting your children in the place of feeling they have to make a choice between caring for your date or your ex; you will risk alienating your kids from both your date and yourself.

Avoid always leaving home to date. Include your children sometimes. Play family games; watch a TV movie. The more you work at including your date in the life of your family, the less your kids may suspect and resent your dating and your dates.

Besides, it's important for you as a parent to see how your date will interact with your children. If you marry this person and he or she ends up treating your kids horribly, you will have to make a decision you won't want to face—between child and spouse.

Finally, recognize that your kids are going to be watching your dating habits. Think about it.

9. Build up your children with encouragement and praise. There is a simple rule within the field of psychology: If you want a behavior to recur, reinforce it. Reinforcement can be either praise or criticism. Sometimes a negative behavior is repeated because it was reinforced with criticism. If you want to shape your family, use positive reinforcement; use praise; catch them when they're doing it *right*, and give them a pat on the back.

Learn to focus on the positive, even if it's a small thing like a slightly straightened room, a bed made for the first time in weeks, or a kind word to a sibling. Look for the positive. When you see it, give it praise and support. Use a personal ratio of eight-to-one, positive-to-negative, affirming-to-critical, kind-to-harsh, gentle-to-forceful.

10. Take time out for yourself. You need an occasional time-out for yourself. Get away once in a while, even if only for an evening or a walk around the block. Work at creating occasional "breaks" for yourself, means by which you can temporarily get out from under the pressures, sniff the roses, and recharge your batteries.

The kind of family you have following divorce will depend on the course you set for yourself and your children. Don't just let it "evolve." It will now take some more intentional work to make it happen, but it's worth the effort. Your kids are worth your effort.

SHOULD I EVER MARRY?

It is not uncommon for children to experience so much pain from divorce that they are afraid to marry; college-aged children are frequently known to break off dating or engagement relationships when their parents divorce. Because of this, children need to hear from their parents that marriage is still a worthy thing, and that two mature adults can indeed make marriage work if they decide to do so. Children also need to know why their parents' marriage failed, so they can attempt to avoid the known pitfalls.

This is another reason why it's important for children of divorce to associate with people whose marriages are successful, so they can see how a positively functioning relationship looks, feels, and works.

AM I GOING TO BE STRANGE, REJECTED, OR OUTCAST BECAUSE OF THE DIVORCE?

Most children handle insecurity and feelings of inferiority by internalizing them. Children of divorce frequently fear that they will now grow up being "different" because of the break-up of their family structure and the loss of a parent. After all, "families" are most often defined as being Mom, Dad, and children.

To counter this, the child's self-esteem and self-respect must be fed and nurtured within an atmosphere of support, nurture, praise, and affection. If there is no other message from parent to child, it should be the message that the child is unconditionally loved, respected, supported, and cherished. "I believe in you" is critical to the child's self-esteem and self-respect. One of the most damaging messages a parent can give a child is that the child is loved because of performance, whether that performance is on the athletic field, in the academic arena, or in the home. Kids need to be loved *regardless*, with no string attached.

WHAT IF MOM OR DAD REMARRY?

One of the most difficult relationships historically has been that of the step-parent. The wicked step-mother in the story of Cinderella has roots in more than fantasy. (Step-fathers have their fairy tales too.) Being a step-parent is laden with substantial challenges for *everyone*. It takes time, work, maturity and prayer. Here are some tips:

1. Avoid challenging the children's loyalty to their blood parent. It is difficult for children to allow themselves to

have loving feelings for two "fathers" or "mothers." They fear that love for one may be at the expense of love for the other, and the fear prompts guilt.

As a step-parent, give full support to the children's ongoing contact with the absent parent. Help the children understand that now they have two adults who love them as a father or mother, but *never* ask the child to make a choice between loving one at the expense of the other.

2. Avoid the too-much-too-soon syndrome. The fact of a new marriage and a step-parent does nothing to change the child's past. The child will still have certain ways of responding to stress, authority, relationships, love, and discipline. Don't expect the child to change instantly and reflect the new values, methods, or family system of the step-parent. It takes time, and the more pressure applied, the greater may be the child's resistance and resentment.

Overnight changes don't happen. Don't expect them. If the new step-parent has new rules or expectations, communicate them plainly and give the child time to make the emotional adjustment to the new situation before demanding compliance.

Young children associate size with authority and power. Consequently adults can often get their way simply by virtue of being bigger. This is not necessarily going to win a child's affection. Excessive use of power usually creates enemies, and it's almost always damaging to the child's self-esteem.

3. Seek to provide additional love, time, and support. In remarriage the emphasis should be on nurturing, supporting, affirming, and giving *more* love and *more* time to the family. Again, focus upon positive goals, positive reinforcement, praise, active encouragement, and as much genuine affection as the children will accept.

4. If discipline or punishment is needed:
   a. Treat children of both sides of the step-family as equally and fairly as possible. (The kids will normally

test these boundaries, to seek a "family advantage" over the other side. Be sure there is none.)
  b. Spend as much extra time as may be necessary to thoroughly communicate family standards and expectations; always frame them in positive statements. ("This family stands for treating people fairly, and it stands for being kind and supportive.")
  c. Praise openly and often; correct privately and gently.
  d. Be sure that both parents always discuss any discipline or punishment.
  e. Avoid the temptation to win a child's support or favor by permissiveness. Stick to your standards and build on the relational things, or you'll create a monster.
5. Before considering remarriage (and step-parenting):
  a. Talk with two or three couples who have already done it. Discuss their experience and struggles.
  b. Talk at length with a professional regarding family issues with which you *will* be dealing, like it or not.

Other issues, including a weekly family time together, where you will live, blending families of varying faiths or family approaches, are also important to address. Talk about everything as a family unit. Learn to make decisions as a family. Avoid creating a dictatorship of any kind, or you'll soon have a civil war, as sides join up to create their respective power bases.

According to many experts, step-parenting and step-family issues are the greatest factor responsible for second marriage failure. Again, if you're thinking of creating a step (or "blended") family, don't do it naively. There are many books available. Do some reading. Be prepared.

HOW KIDS OF DIFFERING AGES RESPOND TO DIVORCE

I give special thanks for much of the information in this section to my very able administrative assistant, Barbara Schiller. Barbara, who has worked with single parents and their children for many years, is the best resource I know for the information that follows.

All the items in the categories below are generalizations. No two children go through the experience of divorce in the same manner. All of the symptoms listed may be present in one child, and few or none in another. But these characteristics are common among children in each age grouping.

Ages Birth to Two Years

1. Have no conscious memory. Not having use of language, infants don't consciously remember events.
2. Have "feelings" memory. They carry memories within the unconscious.
3. Sense confusion. With Mother and Father seen as "one functional unit," when one suddenly disappears the infant is confused.
4. Sense attachment anxiety. Infants need constant affirmation, touching, nurturing. A "disappeared" significant person creates a vacuum.
5. Fear abandonment. Very little research has been done in this area (infants and divorce), but many strongly suspect that this fear is present and powerful.
6. Delay processing. Many of the issues of divorce as experienced by infants will not be addressed until many years later, perhaps even as late as middle adulthood.

Ages Three to Five Years

1. Experience shock. "How could this happen? Where did Mommy/Daddy go? Why?"
2. Fear abandonment. Terror that Mommy will leave just as Daddy did, or vice versa, and child will be alone and helpless. Fear of rejection.
3. Experience attachment anxiety. "I miss Mommy/Daddy so much. I want to cry all the time."

4. Begin to assume personal responsibility—the feeling that somehow, for some unknown reason, they were responsible for the divorce.
5. Can tie memory to words. "I remember the day Mommy/Daddy left."
6. Feel guilt as predominant emotion.
7. Exhibit symptoms of clinical depression, including inability to sleep, disorganized behavior, hyperactivity.
8. Have nightmares.
9. Regress in behavior—bed wetting, thumb sucking, "baby talk."
10. Exhibit psychosomatic symptoms—tummy aches, head aches, throwing up, lower tolerance to colds, flu, etc.
11. Fantasize that parents will remarry; symptom of child's denial of reality of divorce.
12. Are jealous of parents' dating partners.

Ages Six to Eight Years

1. Feel shock. "I can't believe this is happening!"
2. Feel sadness as predominant emotion.
3. Feel overall sense of alarm. Fear of starvation since the breadwinner (in most cases) is gone.
4. Are clinically depressed.
5. "Zone out"—mentally retreat to a "different place," so as to escape the pain of reality.
6. Exhibit aggression—attempts at expressing rage.
7. Feel intensely deprived.
8. Are disorganized.
9. Regress in behavior.
10. Suffer insomnia.
11. Feel vulnerable and frightened.
12. Exhibit denial. "Everything's going to work out okay."
13. Have school problems; "act out" feelings; regress socially and academically; math skills especially difficult (they represent pure logic, and the child's mind is in chaos).
14. Exhibit anger—often directed toward mother (regardless of who custodial parent may be).

Ages Nine to Twelve Years

1. Feel shock.
2. Feel "conflicting loyalties"; fear having to choose to love either Mom or Dad.
3. Feel anger as predominant emotion.
4. Regress in behavior; act out.
5. Hyperactive—representing inner turmoil.
6. Feel personal responsibility for parents' divorce.
7. Fear abandonment.
8. Exhibit anger, directed toward mother.
9. Have school problems—behavioral, academic, and social dysfunction; math skills continue to be major problem.
10. Have profoundly shaken sense of self-identity.
11. Exhibit psychosomatic symptoms—illness or pain, due to lowered resistance to illnesses, a product of stress and anxiety.
12. Exhibit anger toward parents' dating partners, seen as interlopers.

Ages Thirteen to Sixteen Years

1. Feel shock, followed by anger, often aimed at mother.
2. Attack verbally in anger.
3. Attach to cross-sex peer, frequently with sexual acting out.
4. Have school problems.
5. Assume less personal responsibility for divorce.
6. Regress in behavior.
7. Feel anger as predominant emotion.
8. Feel deep sadness and sense of loss.
9. Talk to peers rather than to parents.
10. Feel isolation. Potentially dangerous at this time due to this age group's suicidal tendencies (number two cause of death in this age bracket).
11. Emotionally distance themselves to protect themselves from pain. Makes them vulnerable to sex and drugs.
12. Feel "trapped" in the middle between parents.

Note: If young teens open up to you, don't be shocked at what they say.

Ages Seventeen and Above

1. Sense bereavement profoundly.
2. Verbalize anger and blame against parents. "You are so irresponsible, hypocritical, and self-indulgent!"
3. Are angry with destruction of home they assumed would be there for them.
4. Withdraw from, or wildly abandon themselves to, romantic/sexual relationships.
5. Accept no responsibility for their parents' divorce.
6. Seek neutrality. Want to be on neither parent's side.
7. Play multiple roles. In one day a student, Dad's therapist, Mom's escort, and little sister's "father."
8. Radically alter attitudes toward marriage—for good or for bad. May plunge suddenly into romantic relationships or suddenly break long-standing engagements. Profound fear of marriage.
9. Fear being destined to repeat parents' mistakes.
10. Turn to siblings more than to peers.
11. Exhibit symptoms of clinical depression, including escape into drugs, romantic relationships, food, sleep, work, or any other available source of respite.

No matter what the age of your child, note substantial personality change, behavioral change, or recurring or serious physical illness and seek professional help for your child if any persist.

If you're feeling overwhelmed, hold on. It's one thing to say, "Divorce usually hurts the children." It's another thing to read a long list of symptoms and recognize that one's divorce is responsible for many of those symptoms. Yet giving something a name doesn't give it any more power than it previously had. Listing the symptoms doesn't do anything to increase their power. On the contrary, having information and expected patterns should give you insight so you can more ably address the real issues of your children's lives.

ADULT CHILDREN OF DIVORCING COUPLES

One study found that 25 percent of unmarried adult children of divorcing couples hurled themselves into an intimate relationship within a year of their parents' divorce. They felt the pain and seemingly hoped to end it by an intimate relationship. It's also known that a significant number of *married* adults take precipitous action in their own marriages at or near the time of their parents' divorce.

Young single women are sometimes competitive with their mothers' dating. Young men may become protective of Mom if she begins dating. Older children, seeing the date as a potential sexual partner for the parent, often resent the intrusion. Adult married children often report struggling to accept, even tolerate, a new spouse with the parent at family gatherings.

Following the divorce of their parents, young adult children of both sexes are reported to look at Dad more in terms of his money and power than in terms of his parental role. Because of this older fathers sometimes report losing a special connection with their kids and find themselves held at an arm's length. On the other hand, sometimes it takes divorce before parents can stop fighting each other and focus more energy on their relationships with their kids.

Older children frequently report feeling trapped between warring parents—unable to fully support either and angry at the parents' insensitivity to the adult children's feelings *as children*.

LET YOUR CHILD BE A CHILD

Your child isn't an adult and shouldn't be treated as one. Many children who see their parents in pain feel they must "parent the parent." Sometimes hurting parents encourage this, looking to their children for comfort. As a parent, try not to turn to your children as a primary source of comfort or advice. Don't use them as a sounding board. Don't try to make your children into your therapists or your confidants. Let the child be a child.

Recognize the children's stress levels and don't compound them. Avoid multiple losses, such as school chums, neighborhood friends, familiar surroundings. That is, if you are at all able, continue to live in the same neighborhood after divorce. If you can't stay in the same house, try to rent an apartment close by, in the same school district.

Yes, divorce is painful but the pain is not the final word on the story. Children continue to model their lives after their parents' behaviors even after divorce. As your children watch you deal with their your own pain and healing, as they watch you turn to God for healing, forgiveness, and growth, they will learn from you patterns of recovery.

Finally, here's something worth memorizing:

> What we grow up with, we learn.
> What we learn, we practice.
> What we practice, we become.

What you are, as a parent, will to a large extent be what your children will become. How you handle your divorce, your relationship with your ex-spouse, and your relationship with your children, will teach them how to handle major difficulties in their own lives. The role of parenting never ends. It just changes form.

QUESTIONS FOR REFLECTION

1. How well do you feel your children understand the issues on both sides of the divorce?
2. Review the stages of grief, presented in chapter 1. What symptoms of grief can you identify in your children? In which stage is each? Trace their progress through the grief cycle, looking at their behaviors, attitudes, and relationships.
3. How are your children expressing any feelings they have regarding the divorce? Are they expressing their feelings verbally, or are they acting them out? If the latter, what actions might be associated with what feelings?
4. Identify your greatest concern regarding your children's visitation times with your ex.
5. In what ways have you and/or your ex-spouse attempted to manipulate your children's feelings and affections?

How might these attempts affect your children's ability to love and trust?

6. What is your child's greatest fear regarding growing up in a single-parent household? What is your greatest fear regarding being a single parent?
7. How adept are you at motivating and correcting your children using praise and encouragement? Do you tend more to use negative or positive reinforcement?

ACTION ITEMS

1. Ask your children this week if they have any unanswered questions about the divorce. To the best of your ability, give them honest answers, tempered with love.
2. Observe your children this week and see if you can "tune in" to their feelings as expressed in their behavior. Then tell them what you think you have seen and ask them if you're on target. If you are, ask if they could help you understand a little more about the "why" behind the particular feeling or ask them to describe the feeling.
3. Use one evening this week for participatory "family entertainment." (Don't go to a movie or watch TV.) Play a game, go for a walk, do something that will promote conversation and enjoyment of one another.
4. Take an hour this week with your family and together write down a few things that "this family stands for." Talk about it and see how you can shape your family identity using the list.
5. Talk to one single parent this week and express some of your concerns regarding single parenting. Ask for insights and input.
6. If your children are adults, ask them how you can help them with their divorce-related issues. (Be willing to accept a request for you to back off and let them struggle through this without your manipulation.) Ask how you can best show your love for them.
7. For one week monitor your interactions with your kids, looking for your own positive-to-negative ratio. Make

corrections in your ratio as appropriate, seeking an 8-to-1 ratio, positive to negative.

FOR SPIRITUAL GROWTH

1. Read Matthew 11:28–29. Reflect upon how this text might apply to the single parent and to children of divorce.
2. Read John 4:43–54. What "test of faith" did Christ give the official? What might be some "tests of faith" awaiting you in the week ahead?
3. Attend church together this week as a single-parent family. If possible, sit together and worship God. In the car on the way home, discuss what it means to worship God as a family.
4. Read Mark 5:22–43. How gently do you imagine Christ spoke to the little girl? How can you help your children see the love Christ has for children?
5. As you set new family standards, review Matthew 5–7. How might you incorporate some of these standards and values into your new family identity? What immediate and then long-term impact might they have on your family?

‡

CHAPTER 8

BUT CAN WE COMMUNICATE?

We finally lost all ability to speak to one another rationally. We both got so defensive, angry, and manipulative that nothing we said to each other made sense anymore. There was no longer any such thing as trust.

No matter where you are at this point in your healing—seeing the possibility of reconciliation with your ex or moving on to new horizons—your communications skills are critical to building healthy relationships. With your children, your family, your co-workers, your same-sex friends, any potential future mate.

You may think you're good at it, but communication is an extremely complicated exercise. It is not simply the use of words to express facts or even feelings. If it were, then one could have excellent communication with a well-programmed computer. "Hi!" (Beep.) "How are you today?" (Beep.) "I'm fine, thank you." (Beep.) As a matter of fact, words frequently represent the least significant portion of communication.

It is a multilevel activity with meanings often being more accurately expressed in facial expressions, body language, or tone of voice than in simple use of words. What I meant to say may not be what I actually said, and then there's what your "filters" heard me say and how my "filters" understood your response. Then there are the real facts, which neither you nor I may know or be honestly facing.

Talk to most any counselor, and you'll hear that communication is a critical problem when marriages break up. He thought that she thought that he said. . . . Power struggles may shut off one's ability to hear or speak anything other than venomous words.

It's no surprise to learn that most divorcing people sincerely believe that their spouse never listens to them, that their marriage has serious communication problems, and that the problem is mainly the other person's responsibility. Marriage counselors see a common scenario: "I know I might be responsible for *some* of our communication problems, but you should see how my husband/wife reacts every time I really try to communicate."

THE AWARENESS WHEEL

There are many important "pieces" involved in any interpersonal communication, many dynamics working simultaneously. Understanding these dynamics can help you see the complexities of any relationship.

Consider the visual picture presented in the following Awareness Wheel.[1]

For clarity, let's discuss the parts of the wheel.

Fact or Sense Statements

We looked at facts—as separate from thoughts or feelings—in chapter 2. There's no debating them. Facts are facts. Problems arise when two people don't know the same set of facts or don't confirm what set of facts the communication centers on.

Interpretations, Thoughts, or Perceptions

Every fact can be interpreted into thoughts, but every person will interpret a fact differently. Autumn is autumn. Some people love the changing colors and cooler temperatures; others dislike the season since it represents the end of summer and the

The Awareness Wheel

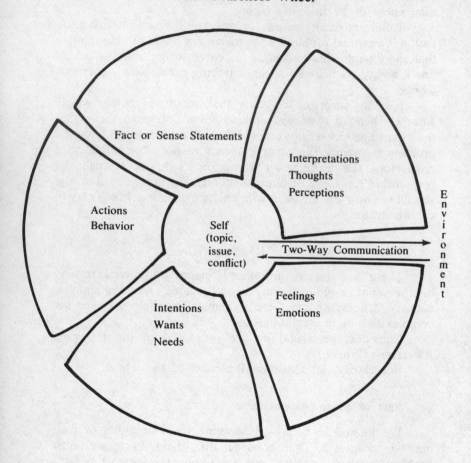

The Awareness Wheel. Copyright © 1991 Interpersonal Communication Programs, Inc. Used with permission. For more information on the uses of the Awareness Wheel and related talking, listening, and conflict resolution skills, call Interpersonal Communication Programs, Inc., 1-800-328-5099.

height of hay fever. Facts are seen through an individual grid of personality, values, and personal history.

Your interpretation of someone else's actions depends on your past history with that person. It also depends on your own mood, even your relations with your childhood family.

Feelings

Feelings usually affect decision making and thoughts, even if subconsciously. Those who rely most on pure fact and logic are often the ones most afraid or least trusting of their own feelings. Some people speak rashly or make decisions based purely upon how they feel, which can complicate communications, as they might feel differently the next day.

In a purely reasonable world, feelings about a certain issue can be tied to facts and interpretations. "I know fall is coming again" (fact). "Fall is enjoyable, with its cool weather, changing colors, and logs in the fireplace" (interpretation). "I feel accepting and eager toward fall's arrival" (feeling).

Intentions, Wants, or Needs

We walk into most conversations with some agenda in mind at least subconsciously. We want something—information, comfort, clarification, or simply a chance to interact. Our wants or needs are substantially colored by facts, interpretations, and feelings. If you think about it, you'll note that you probably tend to judge yourself by your intentions. As far as you're concerned, what you meant to say is what you said—even if what you meant to say wasn't understood as you had wished.

Actions

Our behaviors play out our perception of facts, our feelings, and our intentions. We judge ourselves by our intentions; we judge others by their actions or their behaviors, which include their words and their nonverbal communication. Whether the words or "silent" behaviors are yours or someone else's, what significance do they have?

Choice of words. One's choice of words can trigger a negative reaction, especially if the intent of the word is to create harm. Compare these two examples—two couples confronted with the same "problem." One couple uses "hot button" words to transform a simple communication into a power struggle.

Man: Hey, chubby, has the newspaper come yet?

Woman: You need the exercise; go see for yourself. (Both are telling the other that they wish the other would lose weight. The newspaper is just an excuse for this phase of the battle.)

Man: Has the newspaper come yet?

Woman: I haven't looked. Could you check? I'm tied up with the kids' breakfasts right now.

This second conversation isn't loaded with fiery words, but addresses the facts—to provide information and clarification.

Tone of voice. But a word can have completely different meanings, depending on the inflection and tone of voice, which often carries its own "real" message. For example, let's use two simple words: *nice* and *dress.*

"Nice dress," he hissed, as she showed him her most recent purchase.

"Nice dress!" he said, as he nodded with warm approval.

"Nice dress," she said coolly, as she enviously critiqued her sister's outfit before her sister went to the dance.

"Nice dress," she said, as she marveled at the latest style.

In the first example, the "real" issue is probably money; she spent too much money on a dress. In the second example, he really likes how the dress looks on her and wants her to know it. In the third example, the sister is expressing envy and maybe even a "put down." In the fourth, the woman is impressed with the style of the new outfit. All use the same words, but the message is different in each case.

Nonverbal speech. Those who study human communication often say that up to 80 percent of all communication is conducted not in what words are said, but in the way they are delivered. This might include tone of voice, but it also includes body language—actions that can speak loudly. Is your posture rigid or soft? Are you leaning toward the person you're talking to or away? Are arms crossed rigid around your chest? Is your facial expression open and smiling or stone-cold? Can you look someone right in the eye?

Even if your intentions are warm, others will make judgments based on your actions. As Marshall McLuhan said in the sixties: "The medium is the message"; the way the message is delivered is the message itself.

Self

At the center of the Awareness Wheel is the self, which also encompasses, in this definition, the topic, issue, or conflict at hand. This is the nerve center, the command post that communicates with the environment or the rest of the world. But by the time it communicates to the environment, its communication is powerfully altered by facts, interpretations, intentions, feelings, and choices of behaviors or actions.

As you consider the Awareness Wheel in terms of your own communication, ask these questions:

1. What are the facts:
   - as I see them?
   - as the other person sees them?
   - as they probably really are?
2. What interpretations of these facts might be influencing:
   - myself, given my personal history and personality?
   - the other person, given his or her history and personality?
3. What feelings or emotions:
   - am I feeling as I communicate with this person?

  - is the other person likely feeling as he or she communicates with me?
4. What intentions, wants, or needs:
  - am I attempting to achieve or meet?
  - is the other person attempting to achieve or meet?
5. What behavior or actions:
  - am I acting out (both verbally and nonverbally)?
  - is the other person acting out verbally and nonverbally?
6. What is the issue around which the two of us are doing this "communications dance"?

The Awareness Wheel is an excellent tool to help one "tune in" to the various levels of communication if one wishes to analyze and fine tune messages being sent.

DID I HEAR WHAT YOU SAID?

We've established that communication is complicated. (Did I say what I meant to say?) But dig deeper in considering that communication is between two (or more) people, a speaker and a listener.

Listening and Feedback

The words of the most articulate speaker can easily fall on "deaf ears," if a listener isn't tuning in to hear what is being said.

Someone who's not listening lets his or her mind drift, perhaps formulating arguments or opposing thoughts while the other person is still speaking. It usually includes inaccurate feedback and limited eye contact.

When two people are arguing, they are usually listening in a passive, not active, nature. They hear what they want to hear, not what's actually said. Consequently both parties leave the conversation convinced that the other wasn't really listening.

Giving feedback—checking and confirming—for clarification is a vital part of good communication. Did I understand you correctly? Here's a silly example of two older women on a tour bus in England:

First Woman: I say, Gladys, isn't this Wembly?
Second Woman: No, deary, Thursday.

First Woman: Well, yes, love, I could use a drink.
Second Woman: Brink? On the brink of what, war again? I certainly hope not!

It's obvious that neither woman heard what the other was saying. Much—too much—of what is called communication is like that. To communicate well, provide feedback—and ask for it of others. As important as this is in amicable communication, it is doubly true for parties in the throes of conflict.

Feedback can be verbal or nonverbal. It can be seen in a smile and a nod, or in a cold shoulder and silence. Both communicate very effectively. In fact, if you have to choose between believing one's words and one's actions, believe the actions, as they're usually the more accurate.

PROBLEM SOLVING AND COMMUNICATION

Communication is essential to conflict resolution. Even the best of marriages have occasion for conflict. In their book *Talking Together*, Miller, Nunnally, and Wackman list some of the more common areas of conflict even in healthy marriages:

identity	productiveness	control
career	goals	together/apartness
housing	death	similarity/difference
values	trust	cooperation/competition
opportunities	sex	boundaries
health	commitment	decision making
faith	affection	responsibilities

To their list add the following:

in-laws	holiday traditions	vacations
finances	child-rearing issues	use of alcohol

A simple conflict-resolution formula is used by professionals varying from therapists to management and union negotiators. For purposes of this book, we'll call it the problem-solving formula.

Ask for the Feelings of the Other Party

If Mr. Spock of "Star Trek" lore were told to ask for the feelings of the other party, he would probably respond, "But Captain, that's not logical." The assumption behind his approach is that feelings, which are not logical, should not be trusted. But the fact of human life is that feelings control all decision making and all communication.

Therefore, to open the door to problem solving, begin with the other person's feelings. Be genuine. "What are you feeling right now? What do you feel about this issue?" Be careful of your intentions. If you ask the other person to express feelings only as a tool to get him or her to listen to yours, you will fail in communication. Your goal is solving the problem, not winning the argument. If your intention is to win, you might stop and ask yourself if perhaps the greater part of the problem is your need to win. (You probably thought it was the *other* person's need to win!)

Ask the other person to identify specific feelings—anger, sadness, fear, loneliness. Help the other person get as close to real honesty and vulnerability as you can. The other person will probably "read" your real intentions and allow you as close to the real feelings as trust allows. If you have a past history of being untrustworthy with others' feelings, trust may take time.

Ask the Other Person to Define the Problem as He or She Sees It

Perhaps the problem has already been addressed in the expression of feelings. Or perhaps the feelings are so strong and varied that the person never really nailed down the actual problem. At this point, ask the other party to write the problem down on paper.

Stick to one issue at a time. Be careful—the more complex a problem, the more the conversation may drift away from the hottest point, and the more each party might cloud the issue by bringing more issues into the conversation. Stick to one issue at a time, and don't try to resolve anything yet. Just define issues for now.

If you have listened attentively and politely to the person's feelings, you may now be privileged to "see" the problem from the other's point of view.

If you are the party who wins most of the arguments in a relationship, this will be a difficult process. Problem resolution is frequently a delicate process. Be careful to avoid using your anger, fear, sadness, or any other emotion to control the conversation; you can easily destroy what has just been built.

If you are the party who loses most arguments, now is a good time to say to the other person that it is only fair that he/she now listen to you. Be firm.

Express Your Own Feelings

Be careful to use "I feel" rather than "I think you" messages. Be aware of your feelings and express them as such. From these examples you might see how "I think you" messages can be counterproductive, making the other person defensive.

1. I think you are selfish.
2. I feel left out in much of this relationship.

1. I think you don't love me and never did.
2. I feel sad that you might not love me. I feel scared that I might be unlovable.

1. I think you enjoy hurting me.
2. I feel angry when you hurt me.

1. I think you are unfeeling and invulnerable.
2. I feel scared and exposed when I'm around you.

1. I think you spend too much time at the office.

2. I feel sad because you're more interested in the office than you appear to be in me.
1. I think you spend too much time on the phone with your mother.
2. I feel frustrated at the amount of money spent in long-distance calls, and I feel I'm less important to you than your mother is.

It's always okay to feel what you feel. It's also always okay to express what you feel to the other person. If someone else chooses to use that information to hurt you, that is the other person's problem, not yours. You have been vulnerable; the other person has been calloused. You will live with yourself. Let the other party live with his or her choices.

Define the Problem as You See It

Feelings are wonderful "greased skids" to move even the most stubborn issues out into the light of day. Put your definition on paper. Avoid the temptation to put down how the other person sees it. Be honest about your feelings, and your definition of the issue.

Giving the other party the dignity to express personal feelings and definitions has probably opened the door to genuine interaction. Your listening has set the tone for his or her listening to you.

At this point in the problem-solving process you should have two parties who have fully expressed any feelings about the problem at hand, expressed their individual perspectives, and probably given some insight into individual needs, values, and objectives. Now, and only now, are you both ready to begin problem solving.

Again, a reminder: Avoid use of problem-solving techniques as a means of winning. Your winning means the other person's losing, and the more someone loses, the more that person will need to win the next time an issue arises; the more the other party loses, the greater the alienation and the more ominous the set up for the escalating vengeance cycle.

Create Multiple Solutions

The tendency at this point may be to rush in with your original agenda, "As I said before, if you would only . . . then everything would be all right." Don't! Your solution is probably not going to be seen as a wonderful stroke of genius. In fact, your solution may be seen as an attack, which calls for throwing up barriers and a counterattack; you'll be back to square one again.

Look instead for alternate or creative means of resolving the problem. Work at creating solutions that reduce emotions rather than solutions that allow you to win. Allow each party to come up with alternate or partial solutions. Try starting with ten each. Write them down with no pressure from the other side. It doesn't matter how far-fetched they may be. The objective at this point is to see new possibilities. Be creative. Be a little crazy if you want.

Rate the Solutions

Share your solutions and you should have twenty ideas in front of you. Now rate each, one-to-five: (1) unacceptable; (2) questionable; (3) moderately helpful, but with some problems; (4) helpful; (5) great idea.

Throw out any unacceptable ideas. Both parties have veto power. Nobody may force an unacceptable solution onto the other.

Combine, Edit, and Create a Mutually Acceptable Solution

Finally the time has arrived to solve the problem. Take the list of acceptable solutions or parts of solutions and weave them together to create something fully acceptable to both parties.

If either party is unable to agree on any realistic or acceptable solutions, go back to step one and deal again with feelings. Work through the steps a second time.

Write Down the Solution and Build In Checkpoints

Be sure both sides agree to work toward fulfillment of the solution. Then build in checkpoints, to be sure both sides are doing what they agreed to do. If you wish, add consequences for nonfulfillment of the agreement. Both parties should agree to the consequences. Create consequences that will "mean something" if used.

If things hopelessly break down at any point in the problem-solving process, start at the beginning, with feelings, as they are usually the key to unlocking communication and cooperation.

If you've identified a need for control in relationships, this problem-solving tool will be especially helpful to you as you break down codependent relational patterns. Establishing mutual objectives is more productive than going into the exercise to control or win.

If there are big problems to solve, start with the smaller ones first and build toward overcoming the larger ones after laying a foundation of trust. Incidentally, this process works just as well with children as with adults.

TROUBLESHOOTING FOR PROBLEMS IN COMMUNICATION

It might be helpful to identify specific problem patterns in communication, especially in marriage but also in any relationship.

Control or Power Issues

It is difficult to communicate effectively (and therefore have a healthy relationship with) any adult you are controlling or who is controlling you or with an adult who is not relating to you as a peer—an equal. Perhaps an example might help.

A few years ago my wife and I were seated in a courtroom; an acquaintance was being tried. We were seated on a crowded bench, though there was one empty seat at the far end. Eventually a man we knew inched past us to take that last seat.

He greeted me with a simple "Hello." Then as he passed my wife, he put his outstretched palm on her head and said, "Hi, Marcia."

Later I asked how his approach had made her feel. "I wanted to punch him!" she said. Visualize the symbolic stance, the controlling posture: one standing, one seated; outstretched hand on head—all saying, "I'm bigger and stronger than you. I look down on you. I'll humor you by talking to you, but I don't respect you."

If you are (figuratively) the one standing, reaching down with your hand on the other's head, or the one seated, with a strong hand controlling your head's movement, you're setting yourself up for communication failure—for some form of dysfunctional, codependent relationship.

Peers stand face to face or sit side by side. The unequal approach to relationships frequently elicits anger from the underdog and always keeps the "upper" party from having a real relationship. It's a means of staying in control, in power, and usually ends in relational isolation.

Triangulation

If you and I are in the midst of a serious conflict, I may be tempted to go to your best friend and tell on you. It's called triangulation or relational use of triangles. But it doesn't work. That action on my part will probably make you more angry at me and cause further emotional separation.

If I have a problem with you, I should take it to you, directly, in person. And vice versa. Assuming I will at least give the pretense of listening to you, and you to me, we can probably work things out.

Power or control issues often affect one's desire to triangulate. If I feel less powerful than you and need a back-up force to face you, or if I want to do some damage to your power before talking to you, I might go to your best friend and tell that person what a rat you are. Then I'll have an ally, and you'll have an enemy, and I can rebalance the scales in my favor.

Spouses often do this while going through marital problems or divorce. They go to mutual friends. ("You wouldn't believe what she did to me recently.'') They dump their emotion and accusations on the children. (''Let me tell you about all that your father did to cause this divorce.'')

Triangulation does nothing positive for communication. For me to tell your friend what a jerk you are doesn't resolve anything between you and me. Triangulation in matters of divorce frequently does substantial and long-lasting damage, especially when the third party is a child, being used as a weapon against one of the parents.

COMMUNICATION: AN OPPORTUNITY TO AFFIRM

Do you remember Aesop's fable about the sun and the wind? The wind tried to blow the traveler's cape off, but the traveler only hung on to it more tightly, tying it about himself and closing all the buttons. Then the sun came out and warmed the air so the traveler voluntarily took off his cape. So it is with all communication.

Undergraduate psychology students sometimes learn about human behavior by studying the behavior of animals, including rats. In one study, one maze box was built with an electric grid on the bottom; every time the rat made a wrong turn, it got shocked. In a second maze box, a chunk of strong cheese was placed at the end; every time the rat made a correct turn, the scent grew stronger.

The study found that the rats given negative reinforcement (shocks) for making wrong choices got crabby, quit eating properly, stopped grooming themselves, bit their handlers more often, and fought more with the other rats in their pens. The rats given positive reinforcement (cheese) for making correct choices learned the maze more quickly, ate regularly, groomed themselves properly, got along with the other rats, and were friendly toward their handlers.

We're all ''hungry'' for praise. Most of us are also pretty good at giving ''shocks'' to those we dislike when we see them making wrong choices. What's the point? Within human communication, praise and positive reinforcement bring far more positive responses than criticism.

No matter what your history with someone, you have the

ability to control the communication process from your side. As you work at building rather than tearing down, healing rather than wounding, nurturing rather than cursing, and supporting rather than bashing, the overall communication process with someone will improve dramatically.

Praise opens the doors to further communication; criticism closes them. Praising someone does not mean inventing nice things to say. Rather, it means looking for positive things, even little ones, already present and then reinforcing them. "You look good in that dress." "I like your smile." "Thank you for being thoughtful. I appreciate it." "You cleaned up your room! Thanks!" "Your hair looks great that way." "Great meal. Thanks!" "Thanks for drawing that picture for me." "I like it when you touch me." "I feel privileged to know that you care for me."

As you look ahead to building new relationships, old communications patterns must be broken to allow for healthier interaction. Do you have a tendency to nag at people to try to get them to do things as they think they should be done? (Nagging, "coaching," and criticizing are attempts at codependent control of the other person.) Try rechanneling your energy to applaud and appreciate when things are going right!

Even as you are communicating with your ex, why not make it the most positive experience possible for both parties' sakes? Why not learn to praise, if not genuinely compliment, the other party, at least to learn how to become the type of person who gives praise to others?

If there are children involved, why not learn to use praise and positive reinforcement as tools to help reconstruct deeply wounded self-images and self-esteem levels? Can you think of a single reason why you should not become highly effective in the use of praise as a communication builder? In the end, its use will make you a better person.

QUESTIONS FOR REFLECTION

1. Why does genuine listening become difficult when relationships deteriorate?

2. Think about your communication style. Do you say one thing verbally but communicate another message non-verbally? Explain, giving examples.

3. Have control or power issues or triangulation affected your communication during separation or divorce?

4. How affirming are you perceived to be? How good are you at using affirmation and praise to build relationships? Do you generally use "shocks" or "cheese" in communication?

5. If Marshall McLuhan was right when he said, "The medium is the message," and you are that medium and message, what do you think is being "heard" by:
   a. your ex-spouse?
   b. your children (if any)?
   c. your closest friends?
   d. your parents?

ACTION ITEMS

1. For one week, keep a four-column checklist of all of your significant conversations. Put headings on the four columns: column 1: Name (of person with whom you're communicating); column 2: Subject (of conversation); column 3: Positive; column 4: Negative. Put an x in the "Positive" column for each positive or affirming thing you say in these conversations. Put an x under the "Negative" column for each negative point you make or shot you take. In the next week try to increase your "positives" and decrease your "negatives."

2. Use the Awareness Wheel at least one time in this week, to help you sort through your own communication issues while talking with another person (preferably a friend; start with an easy one).

3. Ask someone who knows you well just how you project yourself in communication. What is it like for them to be close to you?

4. Try to use the problem-solving formula at least once this week, in dialogue with another person, over a specific issue.

FOR SPIRITUAL GROWTH

1. Read Ephesians 4:2–3. How might these verses be used in your communication with your children and your ex-spouse?
2. Philippians 4:4–7 includes several components that directly bear upon communication. What are these components, and how do they work when communicating in a difficult situation?
3. Colossians 3:8–10 gives some very specific advice regarding how not to communicate. What items are listed? Why? What effect would their absence make in communication?

‡

CHAPTER 9

GETTING YOUR ACT TOGETHER

I wasn't sure just who I was any longer. There had been so many changes. I had walked through so much pain and had felt numb for so long. I felt somewhat like a butterfly emerging from its cocoon, but I wasn't sure who this new butterfly would be.

Rebuilding a life after divorce is similar to rebuilding a home after a tornado has ripped it apart and hurled its timbers across miles of open fields.

Let me give you a visual picture of where you've been and where you're heading.

In previous chapters we've walked through stages 2 through 8.

In this chapter let's take a closer look at stages 9 and 10, as you continue to walk toward new wholeness as a single adult.

FAIRLY WELL HEALED, WHO ME?

As you begin to pull out of the cocoon of depression, as you forgive yourself and others, you see that you might have a future. And yet—you still are very aware that a "piece of you is missing." As one divorced person said, "It's as if someone tore

STAGES OF DIVORCE AND RECOVERY

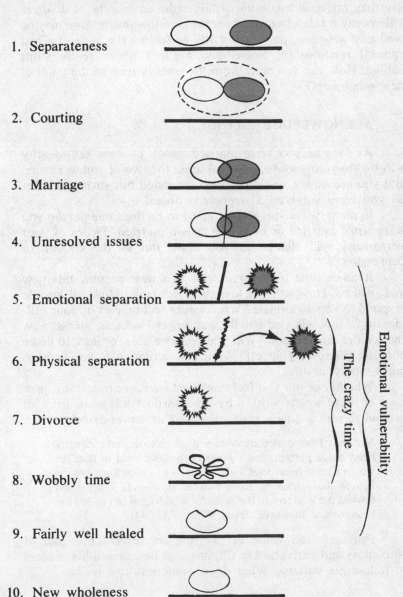

1. Separateness

2. Courting

3. Marriage

4. Unresolved issues

5. Emotional separation

6. Physical separation

7. Divorce

8. Wobbly time

9. Fairly well healed

10. New wholeness

The crazy time

Emotional vulnerability

off one of my arms. The pain is gone, but the sense of loss remains.'' The wound has healed but a scar lingers. Some people say they arrive at this point within eighteen months of divorce. Others say it takes five years for the pain to subside. One may be well past *grieving*, per se, and still be feeling the ache of a lost spousal relationship. Some say the loss never really stops aching. How can you walk from the wobbly time to the point of new wholeness?

ACKNOWLEDGE CHANGE

As long as you were married, much of your self-identity was tied to your spouse. In a real sense the two of you were one. But you are now a single person—wounded but stronger. After all you have survived a wrenching ordeal.

In many ways you are not going to be the same person you were while married or even before you married. Pieces of your personality will change as you crawl out of the cocoon of depression.

It takes time to discover who this new person, this new you, will be. How will you feel about yourself? How will people respond to you as a single? What values will be part of your self-identity? How will you handle fear, anger, sadness, stress, now that you're single again? Will you be more able, or less, to make concrete plans for yourself? What new activities do you want to build into your life?

Whether or not you feel ready to face these questions, take note of these words written by the apostle Paul, who, from all accounts, was a single man, widowed or never-married:

> Not that I have already obtained all this, or have already been made perfect, but I press on to take hold of that for which Christ Jesus took hold of me. . . . Forgetting what is behind and straining toward what is ahead, I press on toward the goal to win the prize for which God has called me heavenward in Christ Jesus. (Phil. 3:12–14)

Paul saw the value of pressing on toward the goal of wholeness and perfection in Christ—and he advised his readers to follow his pattern. What does wholeness involve?

KNOWING GOD

As you rebuild that tornado-destroyed house, turn to the "owner's manual," written by the original Designer, Engineer, and Builder: God. Becoming whole means learning as much as possible about what God wants and doesn't want in human personality and relationships. It means turning one's back on anything that would be opposed to the nature and character of God and walking close to him—every day. It means allowing him to do some housecleaning. It means taking on his characteristics—becoming Christlike.

Here is a list of godly personality and relationship characteristics that I created for myself some time ago. All these items are taken directly from Scripture:

Things God Loves	Things God Hates
Righteousness	Sloth
Justice	Injustice
Humility	Arrogance
Compassion	Getting even
Truth	Slander, tale bearing
Peace and peace making	Grudge carrying
Loyalty	Defrauding via law suit
Faithfulness	Dealing falsely
Gentleness	Meanness, roughness
Hunger for goodness	Self-righteousness
Mercy	Pride
Purity of heart and mind	Impurity of heart or mind
Forgiveness	Unforgiveness
Healing	Destroying
Patience	Impatience
Knowledge of God	Ignorance of God
Lovingkindness	Oppression, extortion, power plays

As you draw close to God ask him to help you redefine who you are. What values and standards are nonnegotiable? As you and your children may have written a family-identity statement,

do the same for yourself: "I am [name] and I stand for
_____." Use the list above to start your thinking process.

KNOWING WHO YOU ARE

"Know thyself" is valuable advice in many ways, the first
being that you need to remind yourself that you are a child of
God, the perfect Parent—the parent you may have always
wished you had (in the flesh). If your mother or father let you
down, know that God will not. He does not reject his children
when they trip—or are tripped.

> The Lord is compassionate and gracious,
> slow to anger, abounding in love [lovingkindness]. . . .
> As a father has compassion on his children,
>   so the Lord has compassion on those who fear him;
> for he knows how we are formed,
>   he remembers that we are dust. . . .
> But from everlasting to everlasting
>   the Lord's love is with those who fear [respect] him,
>   and his righteousness with their children's children.
>
> (Ps. 103:8, 13–14, 17)

In the book of Psalms the word *lovingkindness* is used more
frequently than any other word to describe the character of God.
Can you imagine a loving and kind parent who would hate and
reject his or her own child for any reason? I can imagine a loving
parent grieving because of the child's pain. And that's how I see
God, grieving with you over your pain.

King David made his way through terrible suffering and
bouts of depression by turning again and again to the Lord—his
rock, his fortress. He knew who he was and who made him
whole:

> Whom have I in heaven but you?
>   And being with you, I desire nothing on earth.
> My flesh and my heart may fail,
>   but God is the strength of my heart
>   and my portion forever.
>
> (Ps. 73:25–26)

John says that Christ came to earth—and laid down his life—so that you can have life "to the full" (John 10:10). It's not just a euphemism. As you read and study the Word of God, you will see a marvelous plan of renewal. As you rebuild that tornado-destroyed house, turn to the "owner's manual," written by the original Designer, Engineer, and Builder: God.

Be especially careful to avoid making assessments about yourself without first checking with the Manufacturer, who made you a one-of-a-kind model. You'll find that his assessment of you is more hopeful than your own self-assessment.

TAKING HOLD OF YOUR SELF-ESTEEM

Try saying it, out loud: "I am divorced. I am single. Yet I am unique and completely loved by God. I have a future ahead of me, and I'm going to be all right, especially as I learn to walk close to the Lord."

It may be hard to get the words out. You may be more comfortable with "I'm so dumb. How could I have married the jerk?" "I've always been a failure, and this is just one more example to prove it." "Way to go, stupid. Goofed again."

But you can control the way you talk to yourself. It's a choice. When those negative tapes start rolling, stop them in midsentence. Start playing a new tape—that might be memorized Scripture verses or maybe the paragraph above, at the beginning of this section. Focus your energy on being kind to yourself and talking to yourself words of kindness, gentleness, respect, and acceptance.

You'll reap the rewards in more ways than one. Jesus said, "Love your neighbor as yourself" (Matt. 19:19). Well, that may not be as much a command as an observation: If you can't care for yourself—forgive yourself and look toward the future with confidence—then you can't care for others either. You'll "need" them in codependency, but never truly love them in a healthy long-term relationship.

BUT WHY DID MY FRIENDS LEAVE?

Many people going through divorce say that their married friends were right there with them during the crazy time, but after the dust settled, many of the old friends seemed to fade away.

This is a common reaction that needn't be taken personally. If you related as a four-some, it's just not the same anymore. They may feel guilty sustaining a relationship with you while having dropped your ex. The logistics of keeping in touch with both of you may be difficult.

If you try to keep in touch but it just doesn't work, you may have to grieve these relationships as you move on to others. As you grow toward wholeness, be assured that there will be others. (And look at your situation carefully. You probably haven't been abandoned by everyone—though it may feel that way.)

ON THE ROAD TO A BETTER YOU

Some people find self-assessment lists helpful. Actually write down lists of things that are good about yourself and things that could use improvement. (These provide goals for you to work toward.) You might also turn to friends and ask them how they see you. What do they see as your gifts or strong points? They may offer invaluable help as you begin this process of knowing who you are and rebuilding your life.

As you work through the following list of questions, write your answers down on paper. Reflect on what you write. Get to know this new emerging you:

Personal Checklist

- What am I good at? My strengths? (List ten items.)
- What kinds of things do I like doing most? (List fifteen items.)
- At what point in my life did I most like myself? Why?
- Who likes me, and why do they like me? (Name ten people.)
- What do I have that I can offer others? (Name fifteen things.)
- What things make me happy? (Try to name twenty things.)

- What kinds of things do I do that sometimes hurt relationships? (Name ten things.)
- How can I maintain relationships without harming them? (Name ten thoughts.)
- How many people can I now call "good friends," people who are there for me when I need them?

Emotions Checklist

- How do I handle anger? By attacking, withdrawing, listmaking, pouting, whining, arguing, blaming? Or have I learned to resolve my anger in constructive and positive ways?
- How do I handle fear? By withdrawing, transferring to anger, running away, being aggressive? Or have I learned to turn my fear into constructive motivation; can I use it for energy to succeed?
- How do I respond to stress? By getting tense, frazzled, angry, by controlling others or being out of control, by overcompensating or quitting? Or have I learned to handle stress in ways that reduce it and don't harm me or my relationships?
- How do I handle my own strengths? By boasting, showing off, manipulating others, hiding my strengths, denying I have any? Or do I use my strengths to build healthy self-esteem and relationships?
- How do I handle my weaknesses? By hiding them, denying them, hiding behind them, becoming a weak person? Or have I learned to improve myself in my weak areas, so that I might be a more whole person, more able to enjoy healthy relationships?
- How does my spiritual growth affect my relationships? Does it improve them or make them worse? Does it make me more loved or more rejected? Why?

Relational Attachments Checklist

One of the most helpful and yet most threatening questions to ask oneself has to do with the type of person one attracts as friends. Many times we are unable to see ourselves accurately because of the blinders we wear, but we sometimes can catch a glimpse of *ourselves* by looking at those to whom we may be attracted or those we seem to attract.

- What kind of person is attracted to me? Name five people of each sex. Do they tend to be weak, controlling, sad, unhappy, insecure, compulsive, out of control, impulsive, bitter, frequently rejected, or immature? Or are they mostly happy, secure, gentle, forgiving, comfortable, giving, peaceful, stable, and mature?
- What do I seem to need, or seek, in relationships? Do I seek sophistication, great looks, educational status, financial security, great social or occupational success, or sensuality? Or do I look for openness, genuineness, consideration of feelings, thoughtfulness, honesty, purity, spiritual and emotional stability, and trustworthiness?
- How do I express my desire for close relationships? Does this tack seem to work for me? Do I tend to seek close relationships only with members of the opposite sex? Why?
- How do I want people to respond to me? How does this wish correspond with the way I treat people?
- How do I respond to the praise or criticism of others? Why? How closely is my self-worth tied to their opinions?
- What about me makes people like me? Dislike me?
- What kind of males appeal to me? What kind of females? What can I learn from my choice of either-sex friendships? What do my choices tell *me* about *me*?

Rebuilding your life can be as intentional and well thought out as you wish. If, however, you make no specific goals for your rebuilding, you will fall back into patterns that have led you to this point in your life. You are on your way to wholeness, but five or ten years from now, do you still want to be right where you are today?

"For I know the plans I have for you," declares the Lord, "plans to prosper you and not to harm you, plans to give you hope and a future." (Jer. 29:11)

ESTABLISHING A GAME PLAN FOR PERSONAL GROWTH

Charting a course for your own personal growth will be one of the most important tasks you can undertake as you recover from the trauma of your divorce. Use the outline "Areas for Exploring Personal Growth," on pages 180–84, as a guide for establishing your own game plan. As you rekindle your self-esteem, reaching a few goals will help you feel more in control of your life again. You'll have something to celebrate!

With so many things around you already being in a state of flux, you may find it difficult to muster the desire to face more changes. Remember, take things one day at a time, slowly at first. Each day you can do one or two small things that will gradually improve your circumstances, attitudes, personality, and relationships.

In setting goals for yourself, you will be taking some positive steps, no matter how small, toward creating new, positive circumstances for yourself in the weeks and months ahead. It's a process, not a single event. It begins by taking charge of yourself and your life, deciding where you want to be a month or a year from now, and then aiming yourself, disciplining yourself, toward that objective. Such a process creates personal strength, character, and self-esteem.

MBO (Management By Objective) begins with the objective itself: Where do I want to be in a month or a year? What's the long-term objective?

Once you've established that goal, break the big task down into smaller, more manageable tasks. Set monthly goals, and break them down into weekly tasks. Break your weekly tasks down into daily tasks. Make each daily task simple and achievable. A measurable goal has two benefits: Results are easy to track and you've gained some control in terms of time management: I will swim ten laps twice a week. I will call one friend or family member a day.

After you have accomplished your daily task(s), give yourself a reward. It can be anything you wish—a bubble bath, an ice cream cone—anything. Just stick to the process: Break your big goals down into smaller ones, achieve the small ones one at a time, and then pat yourself on the back. A friend of mine lives by an interesting motto: "Do one scary thing every day." Change and rebuilding can be scary. It's not impossible.

You can see your personal circumstances as opportunities for personal challenge and growth. What you accomplish in facing your circumstances will be a reflection of how well you establish goals for yourself and then how effectively you reach them.

If you do not set goals for yourself, then your circumstances will continue to master you. This moment in your life is an opportunity for growth.

DON'T GO IT ALONE

You'll note that a number of the personal growth areas center on rebuilding relationships—which includes reaching out in trust, which has likely been blown sky high. But you need people. Even if you have lived as a loner, you need people. The "rock" or "island" that Simon and Garfunkel sang of was a pretty unhappy person.

In my backyard I have a competition-sized trampoline, which my three daughters have enjoyed for years. Remember what they're like? A tubular steel frame supports a rubberized mat via scores of strong springs. Most trampolines have four sides and the more springs, the bigger the bounce.

In his book *Bonding*, Donald Joy simplifies the metaphor of E. M. Pattison—that life is a trampoline. He says the four sides represent four different types of relationships:

- Side one: primary family (mother, father, sister, brother, husband/wife, children).
- Side two: secondary family (grandparents, uncles, aunts, cousins, in-laws, nieces, nephews).
- Side three: close friends with whom you're actively connected.

- Side four: exceptionally close friends, including working associates, neighbors you've known for years, high-school or college friends, friends from church, clubs, sports, and so forth.

Trampoline relationships should have the following characteristics:

- There is a high investment in the relationship, with frequent face-to-face contact, and/or by mail or telephone.
- Strong emotional tone characterizes the relationships; you are not indifferent to each other. You would cross the street or spontaneously stop what you are doing to make time for friendly chatter.
- The emotional tone is consistently positive and affirming for both you and the other person.
- The relationship has an "instrumental base." That is, both you and the other person know that in time of emergency the relationship could "cost something" and that you would make the sacrifice to help.
- The relationship is reciprocal and symmetrical. Healthy friendships are so evenly paired that both persons can give and both persons can receive and can do so without "keeping score."[1]

Pattison says that a healthy person should have five or six people on each side of the trampoline—that's a support system of twenty to thirty people.

But, as you undoubtedly know, divorced people are frequently left with the mat (self-esteem) in tatters, many vital springs (close relationships) missing and the frame (one's life) bent.

As you rebuild following your divorce, keep in mind that you need a good, strong system of relationships. If yours is broken, it's time to make plans to repair it.

Consider Dr. Joy's two checkpoints:

First, how many people do we have in our systems? The number is important, since we tend to lose our perspective on reality when the number declines. But a second checkpoint is equally important, namely: are the relationships reciprocal, liberating, and free from a sense of exclusive possessiveness on either side?[2]

An important relational goal at this point is to rebuild your trampoline, to connect again with human beings and move beyond some of your hurt. Friendship, at this point in your life, will be best built upon same-sex relationships.

Following divorce, the very last thing you need, for a long time, is intense male/female relationships. Yes, those relationships are often easier to create, but they're less likely to help you heal. In same-sex relationships there's no romance to cloud the waters and make the relationship seem as if it's more than it really is.

This might be a good time to reconnect with people who have meant a lot in the past—old college roommates, high-school chums, good friends from the old neighborhood. Where are they now? How has life treated them?

If you have real difficulty making and keeping same-sex friends it is very possible that you have some painful and unresolved issues with your same-sex parent. You may have felt competitive with that parent. You may have felt rejected by that parent and may still be in a quest to outdo him or her to somehow gain acceptance. You may have other kinds of issues with that parent, but it's worth your while to grow past this hurdle. You're missing a gold mine of support, friendship, and fun.

Look around you. Not all, but many divorced people, in retrospect, find that they have formed a network of friends who are in some way "wounded"—lone wolves, walking wounded, rescuers, angry types, controlling types, the exceptionally needy or competitive. In healing from divorce it is very helpful to build one's trampoline upon affirming people with good support networks already in place; people who are at peace with themselves and the world; gentle, genuinely loving people who know and walk with God. How do you attract this sort of person? One of the best ways is to become that type of person yourself.

As you rebuild your life, give God room and permission to

grow in you the godly qualities listed earlier in the chapter. Slowly but surely you will enter the stage of new wholeness.

NEW WHOLENESS

Perhaps the chief characteristic of this stage is that you are at peace with yourself, with the world, and with God. One day you wake up and realize that it's been months since you thought about the pain.

This is a morning when you wake and discover that the awfulness of divorce—the fears, the desperate anger, and hopeless sadness—is quite far away in the rear-view mirror of life. It's the morning when you waken and believe, really believe, that life is worth living, and that all those songs on the radio about sadness and being broken aren't worth listening to anymore.

It's the afternoon when you remember that today is the anniversary of your separation, but it really doesn't hurt much anymore. It's the evening when divorce is the subject on TV and you pay more attention to the competence of the actors than to the pain being portrayed.

New wholeness doesn't happen quickly or easily. It happens after the hard work of divorce recovery is behind. You're pretty much self-reliant, functioning well as a single adult. Your new identity is established; your trampoline is stable; you feel comfortable with life. Single parenting has become less frightening, and you have some control of the home front in general. Now you are ready to consider whether or not you want to date.

QUESTIONS FOR REFLECTION

1. How do you think you are seen by others? As being well-kept or sloppy? Intelligent or slow? Interesting or boring? Caring or selfish? Decisive or indecisive? (If you are in a group, ask each group member to offer a personal perspective of you after you have shared your own.)

2. Do you think circumstances reflect the person, or do they create the person? How does this apply to your rebuilding process?

3. Go through the self-inventory in this chapter. Summarize three or four things you learned about yourself.

4. What are the three most frightening items ahead of you as you rebuild? Name them.

5. What is your self-esteem level, and how might it affect future relationships?

6. Give three reasons why it is important to begin building relationships within a framework of being vitally and daily connected to God.

7. Why do some people tend to want to "go it alone" rather than allowing friends to come close and help in the healing process?

8. Give five reasons why same-sex relationships are more helpful than opposite-sex relationships for people going through divorce recovery. Can opposite-sex relationships be trusted during this time of recovery? Why, why not?

ACTION ITEMS

1. Identify two major, long-term goals for yourself. (Example: By this time next year I want to have made six new, good, solid friendships.)

   a. Break those goals down into monthly tasks. (Example: I need to make one good friendship every two months.)

   b. Break those monthly goals into weekly tasks. (Example: I must meet two or three new people each week, get to know them a little and see how the relationship might work.)

   c. Break your weekly tasks into daily ones. (That means every other day I must meet new people. Hmmm, how to do that? Church singles' groups, jogging clubs, political organizations, single-parenting organizations, divorce-recovery groups, church choir, or Sunday school.)

2. If you are stuck and can't move ahead in your healing, set a date for yourself. Write this on a piece of paper, and put it where you can see it daily:
   "On _____ [date] I have chosen to heal from my divorce. I am willing to do whatever is necessary to get on with my life as a new person. Starting on this day I will rebuild! I will identify anything and everything I can that might be of help to my rebuilding, and with the help of God I will do whatever necessary to grow, heal, and rebuild."
   Then sign it and make it your motto.

3. Learn to be nice to yourself. Say at least five good things to yourself, out loud, about yourself, *every day* for a month. Something like this: "When you smile your face brightens up. You are basically a decent person. That sweater looks good on you. You would make a good friend to someone. You are gentle and kind, and I respect you. You are good at many things. God loves you."
   It may take work, but this business of positive self-talk is more than mere psychological hocus-pocus. It's the essence of how God sees us and how he wants us to see ourselves.

4. Draw a four-sided trampoline. On each side, write the names of people who fit the four categories in this chapter. Compare these names with the five characteristics of relationships given on page 175. If you were going to use your friendship network as a gauge of your emotional and spiritual health, how would the gauge read?

5. Given the information you've gained from this chapter, what is the state of your relational trampoline? If it's in disrepair, what do you need to do to fix it?

6. Write a one-page report on what you would like in your next opposite-sex relationship. Can you *be* the person that will attract the person you *want*? What might you need to address (change, modify, mature) in yourself to identify, build, and maintain such a relationship?

FOR SPIRITUAL REFLECTION

1. Read Mark 2:14–17. With whom would you identify most: The disciples? Levi? The religious leaders? The disreputable folk?
   In that setting do you feel Christ would have said he was interested in you or would he have looked away from you to speak to another person in the crowd?

2. Read John 3:1–16. Nicodemus was a religious person, a ruler, and a good man. Why, then, did Christ give him the message of verses 5–8? As you consider your new life as a single adult, what does the concept of new birth mean to you?

3. Read John 11:1–44. What one thing did Christ ask of those who were around (v. 39)? How might this apply to your life? After this event how might Lazarus' priorities have changed? Has divorce changed your priorities?

4. What values does God ask you to stand for? Write a personal statement of your self-identity: [Name] stands for _____.

5. Psalm 15 is a highly relational psalm. What characteristics of relationships are taught? Are these characteristics applicable in our relationships with everyone?

6. How important is it for you to get close to God as you move into your rebuilding stages? What would "getting close to God" mean in your life?
   a. Getting religious and going to church a lot?
   b. Making some big sacrifice, like becoming a missionary?
   c. Starting to pray and read the Bible for thirty minutes a day?
   d. Asking God to heal you and rekindle his presence in your life?
   What's the difference in emphasis between items a-b and c-d?

AREAS FOR EXPLORING PERSONAL GROWTH

I. Spiritual
   A. Moving beyond "religion" into active faith in God.

    B. Reading Scripture to find pieces of God's plan for one's life—and then implementing that plan.

    C. Praying—expecting answers; keeping a daily prayer diary.

    D. Fellowship with other Christians, for the purpose of spiritual growth.

II. Relational (intimate but not sexual relationships)

    A. Stretching "trust" boundaries by opening new parts of oneself to the knowledge and potential impact of another person.

    B. Learning how to *be* at least as good a friend as one wishes others would be; learning what one does that may wound, alienate, offend, aggravate, or in any way keep others away from oneself.

    C. Quitting manipulative behavior.

    D. Asking close and trusted friends for insight regarding how one can become a better friend, a better person, more mature, more stable, more well rounded, and easier to live with.

III. Social

    A. Building one's network (or trampoline) of relationships.

    B. Regularly inviting people into one's life; entertaining; pursuing healthy relationships.

    C. Remembering others' birthdays, sending notes of friendship, etc.

    D. Starting each conversation with a smile.

IV. Physical

    A. Taking care of oneself physically so one can look in the mirror and appreciate what one sees.

    B. Exercise ideas:

1. Jogging	9. Rowing
2. Bicycling	10. Skiing downhill
3. Swimming	11. Playing tennis
4. Lifting weights	12. Playing racquetball
5. Doing aerobics	13. Walking
6. Stretching	14. Jumping rope
7. Walking stairs	15. Doing calisthentics
8. Skiing cross country	16. Playing golf

   C. Taking care of face, hair, nails, muscle tone, weight, heart, and digestion.

   D. Quitting addictive habits, such as smoking or drug use.

V. Healing the Past

   A. Seeking to end any ongoing "wars" with people in the past.

   B. Seeking personal healing for traumatic events in one's past.

   C. Learning how to identify controlling issues from the past.

   D. Reading self-help books, seeking counseling or therapy, going back to those who have caused hurt to seek peace.

VI. Relationship With Family

   A. Rekindling relationships with direct family.

   B. Seeking to heal any wounded familial relationships.

   C. Committing to at least monthly contact with family members.

VII. Professional Development

   A. Identifying next step upward in professional career.

   B. Identifying steps to reach that goal.

   C. Beginning to take initial steps.

VIII. Academic

   A. Continuing education for professional development.

   B. Continuing education for a vocational enrichment.

IX. Food

   A. Identifying ten new types of food never tasted and trying them.

   B. Cooking ten new recipes using unusual ingredients.

   C. Creating new combinations of food, new recipes.

X. Adventure

   A. Deciding to do one scary thing every day.

   B. Taking up parachuting, rock climbing, or rappelling!

   C. Doing something out of the ordinary just to experience it.

XI. Travel

    A. Vacationing in new places (the mountains, the ocean beach, the country; or doing it splashy—Mexico, Canada, Europe).

    B. Traveling in new mode (bicycling, camping).

    C. Visiting each state's major tourist attractions or national parks.

    D. Traveling with a friend.

XII. Hobbies and Recreation

    A. Taking up a new hobby with goal of becoming an expert.

    B. Taking up new hobby with goal of making a profit from it.

    C. Taking up new form of recreation simply for joy of relaxation.

    D. Examples of hobbies/recreation:

1. Stamp collecting
2. Baseball card collecting
3. Learning photography
4. Coin collecting
5. Repairing engines
6. Skydiving
7. Wood working
8. Sewing/knitting/needleworking
9. Bird watching
10. Restaurant sampling
11. Sailing
12. Playing new sports
13. Hang gliding
14. Learning a foreign language
15. Playing bridge
16. Gourmet cooking
17. Upgrading computer skills
18. Writing foreign pen pals
19. Reading a book a month
20. Learning ceramics or other art

XIII. Clubs or Other Organizations

    A. Joining singles' organizations.

    B. Joining political organizations.

    C. Joining sports organizations or clubs (co-ed softball teams, health clubs, tennis organizations).

    D. Attending specialty-organization meetings (reading clubs, travel clubs).

    E. Attending church.

XIV. Personal Self-Esteem

    A. Reading books on building self-esteem.

B. Growing and developing self for purpose of self-appreciation.
C. Forming multiple good relationships to feel connected and appreciated.
D. Making life quest to learn to heal from past hurts.
E. Setting and achieving personal goals.
F. Learning to take personal responsibility for one's life and circumstances.

XV. Developing Leadership Skills
A. Volunteering time and talents to organizations and ministries.
B. Joining Toastmaster's.
C. Reaching beyond one's accustomed limits at work or within organizations.

XVI. Service to Others
A. Growing past one's own self-focus and making a positive difference in the world.
B. Giving of one's own resources (of any kind) to help others in any kind of need.
C. Seeking to use one's own past pain to help make a positive difference in the life of another person suffering from similar pain.

XVII. The Art of Reconciliation
A. Practicing it in one's own life and relationships, no matter what the situation.
B. Seeking to build reconciliation in one's work setting.
C. Learning to recognize need in others and helping them reconcile with those from whom they are alienated.

XVIII. Self-Care
A. Learning how to "nurture," accept, and gently care for oneself—better than anyone else ever has.
B. Making an inventory list of your fears and setting personal goals, with specific steps and timetables, to overcome each fear, one at a time.

‡

CHAPTER 10

BIBLICAL PERSPECTIVES ON DIVORCE AND REMARRIAGE

I was so confused. I felt so far away from God. My church was telling me I was damned. My Christian friends just pulled away from me. I really hurt. Had I committed the "unforgivable sin"? And what about remarriage? For a while I thought perhaps I should just give up and go live with somebody.

There is no doubt that our culture is going through a radical redefinition of values. Some of the changes are dramatic, especially in relation to divorce and remarriage. According to the Bureau of the Census (1988), between 1970 and 1988 the divorce rate increased from slightly less than one out of three marriages to approximately one out of two. But who's shocked any longer to hear of a 50 percent divorce rate?

Frighteningly high marital failure rates—even higher remarriage failure rates—raise a question: Is there any source of stability? Is there any reliable anchor or compass for direction? If one says that God is such a compass or anchor, what help does he have to offer to the divorced person? Is divorce always against God's rules? Is remarriage ever permitted? Is something that is "permitted" also the "right" thing to do?

In one chapter it is virtually impossible to cover the subject of biblical perspectives on divorce and remarriage. The issues are far too complex, and there are too many varying theological perspectives. The primary intent of this chapter is to provide scriptural information, with points to ponder, as you go through divorce and consider remarriage.

THE OLD OLD STORY

Imagine Adam, waking up from a deep slumber, stretching, yawning, picking a fresh banana to eat, and then remembering: *God was going to make a friend for me. I wonder where?* And then he sees her. He's never seen a female human being before, but there she is. Magnificent! Soft curves, wonderful flowing hair, pendulous breasts, an absolute wonder—the first ever! And she looks at Adam—strong wide shoulders, rippling chest, straight, keen gaze, thighs like tree trunks. And they both, in the same instant, gasp and say, "You're beautiful!"

> The Lord God said, "It is not good for the man to be alone. I will make a helper suitable for him."
> . . . Then the Lord God made a woman from the rib he had taken from the man, and he brought her to the man.
> The man said,

> "This is now bone of my bones,
>   and flesh of my flesh;
> she shall be called 'woman,'
>   because she was taken out of man." (Gen. 2:18, 22–23)

This relationship of beauty and wonder was to be an exclusive one, so intimate and connected that it would be described as being "one flesh," a single operating entity, bonded, welded together.

> For this reason a man shall leave his father and mother and be united to his wife, and they shall become one flesh.
> The man and his wife were both naked, and they felt no shame. (Gen. 2:24–25)

Not many generations back there was no such thing as a marriage license or contract. The marital union was based upon a simple but profound and powerful item: a covenant.

There's a substantial difference between a covenant and a

contract. A covenant is a simple promise made between two parties; we agree to this relationship. That's what marriage is all about. In the beginning marriage was intended by God to be a covenant, a promise: "I commit my life and love to you until either you or I die."

A few thousand years after the concept of the marital covenant was established, the state came along saying that people had to have a marriage license to wed. So the idea of a contractual, legal joining became associated with marriage. Contracts are made to legally ensure performance up to expectation and/or delivery of goods or services. A contract can provide a helpful framework within which two or more parties exist, but a contract is a sad replacement when used as an alternative to a covenant, a simple but lifetime-binding promise: "Until death do us part." (The church's role has been to recognize and affirm the holiness of that promise, to solemnify it, and to place that conventional relationship within a loving and supportive community.)

BROKENNESS

All was well in the Garden of Eden, until Adam and Eve chose self-gratification over obedience to God. From that point the history of humanity has been littered with examples of what it meant to "fall." Stealing, cheating, lying, rape, murder; wars, famines, earthquakes, floods; holocausts, mass destruction—the litany is like an unending horror film.

Include divorce in that litany. God's original intent was a study in perfection and simplicity: one man, one woman, a single operational unit, sharing everything from hearth and bread to feelings and sexual intimacy. But the beautiful picture got wrecked and covenants were broken.

Dealing with the realities of the fallen world, God gave Moses divorce laws. Not many. Just a few, found in Deuteronomy 24:1–4. Basically they say that if a man wants to divorce his wife (and the reason for that desire is vague), he can give her a certificate of divorce (note: to break a covenant God asks for a contract) and send her out. If either remarries and then divorces again, they can't remarry each other. That's basically the divorce law given in the Old Testament.

It may sound unfair to women, until one understands that the rabbis added in their auxiliary writings that a man divorcing his wife had to give her double the dowry she brought to the wedding—so she wouldn't be left penniless.

This law was given within a culture that was absolutely male dominant. In fact, at this point in human development, women were viewed like highly valued property. In this ancient culture, the brokenness of the Fall was being played out, and divorce was granted by God as a concession, a sad nod acknowledging a grievous ink blot upon the lovely picture of innocence, bondedness, and love.

Divorce was never God's intention. I've never met anyone who has said that divorce was a wonderful plan for living a happy life. I've never heard a divorced person say, "Gee, my divorce was so much fun; I think I'd like to have two or three of them." Divorce is a lousy experience. It's ugly, painful, and not anything that one would wish upon another person.

GOD HATES DIVORCE

If you're a parent, imagine watching your child go through an experience that would tear at the child's soul and cause deep and lasting pain. Wouldn't you hate anything that would hurt your child this badly? Most parents would.

Scripture says clearly that God hates divorce. It's not too difficult to understand why. It's not that God hates it because it represents people stepping out of a rigid cage he constructed and in which he demands us to live. Rather, God hates divorce because of what it does to people he loves! He hates the deception, the breach of faith, the long-lasting agony that is part and parcel of divorce. He hates what it does to the children, too, the "God-given offspring" mentioned in this famous text dealing with divorce:

> [God] stands as witness between you and the wife of your youth, the wife with whom you have broken faith, even though she was your partner and wife *by covenant*. Did he

not create a single being that has flesh and the breath of life? And what is this single being destined for? God-given offspring. Be careful for your own life, therefore, and do not break faith with the wife of your youth. For *I hate divorce*, says Yahweh the God of Israel, and I hate people to parade their sins on their cloaks. . . . Respect your own life, therefore, and do not break faith like this. (Mal. 2:13–16 JB, italics added).

A few years ago my youngest daughter had a ruptured appendix, and my wife and I had to drive through the night, from the mountains of central Colorado to a hospital. It is a terrible memory. I hated her pain. I hated the uncertainty as I feared her life was in jeopardy. I hated the ruptured appendix! It's natural for a parent to hate a child's pain. It's natural for God to hate divorce.

A DEEPER LOOK

Despite his hatred of and grieving over divorce, there is some evidence within Scripture that God allows, and even in one case commanded, divorce. Here I'm not establishing a principle in favor of divorce, I'm making a statement in opposition to those who would argue that all divorce in all circumstances is condemned by God.

One time, and only one time, God told a group of people that they were to divorce their wives. The story is found in Ezra 10. It's a sad story, of about a hundred men who had married women outside the Israeli nation. At that time, to maintain Israel's covenant (there's that word again) with God, the people were to marry only within their own nation—to keep the nation intact, avoid worshiping false gods, and keep the Messianic line pure.

To get things right with God again, these 113 Israeli men were instructed to divorce their foreign wives: "Now make confession to the Lord, the God of your fathers, and do his will. Separate yourselves from the peoples around you and from your foreign wives" (Ezra 10:11).

The point is that if God were totally and universally opposed to divorce, he would not have commanded 113 men to divorce their wives. Yet, even in this text, divorce is seen to exist within a painful and difficult situation. One could not argue that the circumstances leading up to these 113 divorces were what God had desired or intended.

AT ONE POINT GOD DIVORCED ISRAEL

It was a sad moment in the history of the nation of Israel, but in Jeremiah 3:8 God, speaking through the prophet Jeremiah, says: "I gave faithless Israel her certificate of divorce and sent her away because of all her adulteries. Yet I saw that her unfaithful sister Judah had no fear; she also went out and committed adultery."

It seems that God understands what it feels like to be betrayed, left for another lover; at one point he realized that there was no hope for the relationship other than to end the covenant with a contract, a writ of divorce. This isn't a place for anger. It's a place for sadness. It's a product of the Fall, of the brokenness of us all.

STILL GOD PURSUED

This may not make much sense, but four verses later God continues to plead with Israel, begging her to return:

"Return, faithless Israel," declares the Lord;
"I will frown on you no longer,
for I am merciful," declares the Lord,
"I will not be angry forever." (Jer. 3:12)

Perhaps this thought is best captured in the Old Testament book of Hosea. In chapter 1, God tells Hosea, a prophet, to go and marry a prostitute. Hosea does so—marries a woman named Gomer. They have two children, and then she walks out on him.

For many people that would be the end of the story: "She cheated on him—that's enough. He should divorce her." But Hosea the holy prophet, the symbol of God to the community, goes out and finds Gomer. She's been arrested for prostitution. In those days such women were sometimes sold into slavery.

She's now on the auction block, probably naked, being sold off like a piece of meat; let the new owners see what they're buying.

And Hosea comes along. Everyone is watching to see how he will react. Will he spit at her? Will he shake his head and walk away? Will he give her a lecture in front of the whole town and then leave the scene in righteous indignation?

No. He buys her back. Not to punish her, but to love her. This gets pretty tender, but if you know anything about love, you know that it doesn't just stop because a partner breaks a promise and steps out on a marriage. The problem is that the pain of loving becomes so severe that frequently a wall has to be erected—a legal contract that says, "You two people aren't married any longer." But talk to those who have lived through their spouse's infidelity, even if they decided they couldn't live with a broken covenant and sought divorce, and many will confide that the heart still aches with love.

Actually the story of Hosea, in which Hosea is a dual symbol, representing both himself and God, and Gomer is a dual symbol, representing both herself and Israel, gets even more painful: Hosea continues to provide for her, and she simply uses the provision for her illicit escapades. I have a hard time imagining any relationship more painful than that—giving money to your spouse and then watching as your spouse uses the money for other lovers.

That's the image of God loving us. That's the "high water mark." It's not the rule. It's not something that God expects us to copy. But it *is* an example of how one can still love one's spouse, even if there is adultery.

SPECIFICALLY MENTIONED GROUNDS FOR DIVORCE

The only universally agreed upon reason given within Scripture allowing for divorce is adultery. It's given as just cause for divorce both within the Old and New Testaments. The reason is not too hard to comprehend: Adultery represents a breach of promise, a breaking of the covenant. It rips at the heart of a relationship, destroying trust and crushing the spirit. Yet God didn't say you *had* to divorce your spouse because of adultery.

This is where it gets really difficult, because each person has his or her own ability to carry on in the face of overwhelming adversity. The point is reached at which God doesn't tell us any longer what we are to do in the face of adultery. Rather, he leads the way and at least shows what *can* be done.

But is adultery the only grounds for divorce? Based on 1 Corinthians 7:11-15, some would also include being left or "abandoned" by an unbelieving partner as acceptable grounds for divorce, giving a person permission to leave the marriage without carrying moral responsibility. And from this passage (v. 11), some would argue that indefinite legal separation is an acceptable way for Christians to end a marriage in which differences could not be reconciled. Some feel indefinite legal separation is better than divorce.

DIVORCE AND SIN

This is a point of great difficulty in this chapter, because it would then appear that all divorce (other than that precipitated by adultery or abandonment by a nonbeliever) is "sin." In fact, some people interpret Scripture in a way that appears as if virtually *all* divorce is sin. This approach, then, leaves many people who were divorced by their mates, people who resisted divorce but in the end had no choice but to accept it, living their lives in a constant state of feeling they are "in sin."

Is divorce sin? Incidentally, what almost always follows such a question is condemnation. "Ah hah! Caught you! You sinned!" If you want to know God's response to being asked to (a) define just what is a sin and (b) isolate and punish the sinner, read again John 8:1-11, where Christ was asked to condemn a woman caught in the act of adultery. Caught! Ah hah!

The assumption was that Christ would either have to condemn her, which was what the religious people wanted, or lose his credibility, which was also what they wanted. (Religious people can be such a pain, sometimes.) Christ responded to them by saying, "Let the one among you who has never sinned throw the first stone at her" (v. 7 PHILLIPS).

He didn't stop to define sin! He didn't lecture her about the evils of promiscuity! He didn't even sigh and say, "Well, I guess you made a pretty big mistake this time didn't you?"

So is divorce a sin? Well, another time when Christ was asked such a question, he said:

> "You have heard that it was said to the people in the old days, 'Thou shalt not murder,' and anyone who does so must stand his trial. But I say to you that anyone who is angry with his brother must stand his trial; anyone who contemptuously calls his brother a fool must face the supreme court; and anyone who looks down on his brother as a lost soul is himself heading straight for the fire of destruction. . . .
>
> "You have heard that it was said to the people in the old days, 'Thou shalt not commit adultery.' But I say to you that every man who looks at a woman lustfully has already committed adultery with her—in his heart." (Matt. 5:21–22, 27–28 PHILLIPS)

Christ didn't like defining sin. Rather, he tried to focus on what was going on inside the soul. What was motivating the person? What was the person's attitude? Behavior itself, used as a measuring stick, can be so deceptive! Christ took the laws from the Old Testament and tightened them down several notches, essentially to help people understand that it is the inside of a person that matters, not merely what they do.

So is divorce a sin? Well, it depends. If marriage is based upon a covenant, a promise, then divorce represents a "breach of promise," or a decision to break that covenant. If one understands that divorce is a termination of a covenant or a breach of promise, then one understands that legislating grounds within which divorce is permissible—defining sin—is somewhat like seeing just how far one can stick one's foot over a chalk line before one is considered out of bounds. Does adultery constitute a breach of promise? Certainly. Does abandonment of one's partner? Of course it does.

But the list can grow. There are scores of ways that covenants become broken and wasted: lying, cheating, power plays, manipulation, selfishness, immaturity. Does alcoholism, in which the "mistress" becomes the bottle and any meaningful relationship becomes impossible, constitute a breach of promise? Does physical beating and/or rape? What about attempted murder of one's spouse? What about the spouse who never speaks to a mate without degrading or in some other way emotionally bashing?

What about the woman whose own personal issues cause her to so dislike sex that she refuses her mate and in effect "pushes" him into someone else's arms? Who's most responsible for the breach of covenant? If clinical theory is accurate when it says that marriage is much like a "dance," with *both* partners being responsible for its success or failure, then who's tripping whom? It becomes apparent that the list for "breach of covenant" becomes too complex to sort out. Indeed, enumeration or list making becomes pointless as one begins to realize that covenants are made and most often broken by both parties to the relationship—not by just one guilty person who did some terrible act.

Again citing clinical theory, for there to be a sadist in a relationship there almost has to be a masochist. To ask who's more guilty for the damage to the relationship is useless.

In the Sermon on the Mount, Christ talked about many products of the Fall, including strife between any two people, lust, swearing oaths, retaliation, hatred of enemies, doing good deeds to gain public favor, unforgiveness, greed, standing in judgment of others. Yes, divorce is in his list. Just like war, rape, and murder, divorce is a product of man's brokenness. And none of these acts or motives, including divorce, is to be taken lightly.

So is it a sin? I would ask why one needs to define it as such. Is it painful? Yes. Is it destructive to everyone involved? Usually. Does it brutalize God's original, beautiful plan? Yes. Does it cause people to hate one another? Usually. Does it create chaos in people's lives? Yes. Does it create a greater tendency to fail again in future marital relationships? The studies seem to say so.

Is divorce something that people would wish for? Not unless they are already badly hurting. Is it constructive to human growth and development? Sometimes—perhaps like having a painful root canal done on a rotten tooth. Is divorce God's intention, his purpose? No, it's certainly not that.

The bottom line of divorce is that it is a product of humanity's brokenness and separation from God. And brokenness needs healing, not religious condemnation. Religious people frequently condemn divorce as sin. God, however, looks at divorce, knows what it feels like to be betrayed, and aches. He offers forgiveness and healing as you open your life up to the work of the Holy Spirit of God who is able to put salve onto the deepest hurts.

WHAT ABOUT REMARRIAGE?

If you have read and understood the chapter dealing with codependency, if you understand that the human personality has an amazing tendency to fall into the same holes (and relational styles) time after time (when you read in a subsequent chapter the high statistics pertaining to second marriage failure), you will begin to understand that remarriage is not necessarily the best bet in the world.

Some Christians believe that a divorced person has absolutely no right to remarry. That position is usually drawn from the teaching of Christ in Matthew 5:32 and 19:2–12, and Paul's teaching in 1 Corinthians 7:6–16. Many other texts may be used, but these are the three most frequently quoted in defense of the absolute position against remarriage.

Yet Deuteronomy 24:1–2 (NASB) says,

> When a man takes a wife and marries her, and if it happens that she finds no favor in his eyes because he has found some indecency in her, and he writes her a certificate of divorce and puts it in her hand and sends her out from his house, and she leaves his house and goes and becomes another man's wife. . . . (italics added)

In this passage God recognized that divorce was going to happen, and also that remarriage was going to happen. It's in Scripture: when a person remarries.

Some would treat this as license to remarry, as if to say, "Whee! I can marry and divorce all I want." That was not at all God's intent, any more than airport emergency crash crews were the original intent when airplanes were first designed. Both represent brokenness, concessions, not original intent. Ideally, one would prefer to use neither.

Remarriage cannot be taken lightly (neither can revenge, hatred, unforgiveness, which Jesus, in Matthew 5 equates with murder). Christ taught that remarriage, in most cases, constituted adultery. Matthew 19 is pretty stiff teaching. Some would debate the difference between an *act* of adultery and remarriage, arguing that remarriage does not constitute a constant *state* of living in adultery. Others would disagree.

The question remains: Will remarriage cause a person to be alienated from God forever? Varying Christian traditions will provide varying answers. I take the position that God is not in the business of hatred, rejection, and criticism. He's in the business of healing and reconciliation. (See the parables of Luke 15.)

God understands us. He created us. "For he knows how we are formed, he remembers that we are dust" (Ps. 103:14). He knows that we're going to fall flat on our faces from time to time. He knows that we are stained with the brush of brokenness— that we put some of that black stain on ourselves, and that some of it was put onto us by our parents, siblings, peers, and others.

Still, there are always consequences when one chooses to live outside of God's best plan. Perhaps the most difficult part of this discussion is understanding that remarriage might *not* be God's best plan for the divorced person. There's something about a second marriage that seems to place it on a different level than a first marriage. For example, in the Old Testament, priests were not allowed to marry divorced women. Other people were not specifically prohibited from marrying a divorcee, but priests could not.

At this point, then, the question becomes: Do I wish to seek what I see as *my* best plan for my life, or will I attempt to reorder my life in accordance with what I think may be God's best plan for my life? In the issue of remarriage, this question is unavoidable. But a decision to remarry will not hinder God from loving you.

As one wrestles through the issue of remarriage there is a central theme: We are known and loved by God, and yet we are responsible for our choices and our actions. God won't stop a bullet going from a pistol into another person's heart; he won't stop one's mouth from telling lies or another person's ears from hearing them; he won't magically make a second marriage work after one has not been able to sustain a first marriage. He has created a world in which we are responsible for our decisions and their consequences. If we choose to drive the knife into ourselves, God does not stop the blood from running.

God gives us instructions as to how life is best lived, relationships made and sustained, and our humanness best enjoyed. Then he walks beside us, as close as we will allow, and helps us mend the heart when it gets broken, salve the wounds when they are ripped into us; he invites us to return home to him when we have run away.

If we come home he'll forgive us and love us, even if we're scarred and broken. If we choose to follow him, he will heal and direct our lives in ways that we could never have imagined.

Everything that has been written to this point does not answer the question: Should you remarry? That question must be addressed between you and God. The statistics regarding remarriage are not encouraging. Scripture seems to be tilted against remarriage, and yet remarriage is allowed within Scripture, as a concession. Remarriage is, at the very least, an issue to be thought through, and prayed through, individually.

SUMMARY

Though our culture is out of control, the old rules having been thrown to the wind, God has not changed, and scientific studies, to the surprise of many, are now beginning to substantiate the wisdom of the biblical position.

Brokenness is the inevitable product of the Fall and humanity's separation from God. Divorce is always a product of brokenness. Scripture says that God hates divorce, and what parent doesn't hate anything that deeply wounds his or her own children?

God is not unfamiliar with divorce. At one time he commanded it in a specific situation. At another time Scripture says he divorced Israel, and yet he immediately sought reconciliation with her.

The example that God gives in Hosea is a profound look into the character of God: He loves even in the face of rejection. It is an example, but such perfect love is not demanded of us.

God allows divorce as a concession to brokenness, though he always encourages reconciliation, healing, and restoration. He specifically allows divorce in cases of adultery and abandonment by an unbeliever. Yet he never commands divorce.

Divorce is a breach of covenant, involving pain and brokenness. It is less important to label something as a "sin," and more important to deal with the issue of the heart causing the problem.

In some ways, focusing upon the issue of "divorce and remarriage" is to miss the central issue: molding one's character to the character of God, thereby being equipped to live peaceably and harmoniously with others. Regardless of how it may be acted out, brokenness—and therefore divorce—is always a spiritual issue that requires spiritual healing.

Remarriage is not what God intended from the beginning, yet within Scripture it is given as an assumed concession in our broken world.

Finally, Scripture never says that God hates the divorced person. The focus of God's action with humanity is always that of forgiveness, healing, and restoration. Though we must live with the consequences of our choices, God continues to walk with us and love us.

QUESTIONS FOR REFLECTION

1. As you understand the content of this chapter, what are some of the major spiritual issues pertaining to divorce and remarriage?
2. How does our culture approach divorce and remarriage different from the more traditional biblical approach?
3. How does God handle the issue of personal responsibility?
4. Considering any brokenness, dysfunction, or codependency that might have been evident in your previous marriage, what practical reasons do you see in the scriptural caution against remarriage?

5. Does God's great love and desire for reconciliation mean that we are now free to fail as much as we please? What are the consequences of such an approach?
6. What is your spiritual perspective regarding remarriage? Does your faith permit you to believe that it is all right for you to remarry after divorce?

ACTION ITEMS

1. Take a personal inventory of your relationship with God. Who's in the "driver's seat" in your life as you know it? In terms of your life and character, what influence does God have upon you? How connected to God are you?

FOR SPIRITUAL GROWTH

1. Read the story in Luke 7:36–50. There are several different characters in this story: the woman rejected by polite religious society because of her personal failures, the Pharisee, his buddies, the woman's lovers, a friend or two of hers, the crowd, the disciples. Which of these people or groups would best characterize you? Why? Was Jesus concerned about defining her sin? What was his concern? Read Psalm 23:5. What is God saying to you?
2. Read 1 John 1:5–10. Reflect upon its message to you in regard to your brokenness and divorce.
3. If you are a single parent, read Psalm 69:1–6. Reflect upon how you and God together might best love and heal your kids.

‡

CHAPTER *11*

DATING AFTER DIVORCE

It's like being back in adolescence again, with all my old insecurities. I never thought I'd feel silly again, like when I was sixteen, but that's how I felt. My kids couldn't believe I was actually going on a date! And have things ever changed since the last time I was dating!

Being divorced opens the door to dating again. Many people never wish to date again. Many are not ready to begin dating for a long time after their divorce, but some can hardly wait to begin. Some struggle with spiritual convictions about divorce and remarriage, and others leap toward the possibility of reattaching. Regardless of what one feels or believes, one thing is almost certain: The opportunity for dating will present itself—so it is wise to think through some things and make some decisions before entering the mainstream.

Here in Missouri there are many clear Ozark Mountain streams, superb for canoeing. Before attempting to canoe through the occasional white-water rapids, the wise person stops and mentally surveys the stream, making decisions about how to navigate and what to do in case of an emergency. So it is with dating. Before going through the rapids ahead, it's wise to stop and ponder. This chapter is written to help you get a handle on what might be ahead.

ARE YOU READY TO DATE?

Though it may seem extreme, the real question may be "Are you ready to remarry?" As a parent you might have told your own children to be wise about whom they dated; they might fall in love and even end up marrying that person. So it is with yourself: You could end up marrying virtually anyone you date.

You've been through it before; once the love feelings kick in and the picture becomes romantically blurred, trying to "talk sense" into a person (including yourself) is pretty hopeless. So when it comes to dating, the best time to use good sense is at the start, before emotions start to color and gain control.

Let's look at some issues that would indicate whether or not you're ready to date—or to remarry.

ARE YOU HEALED AND WHOLE?

If you need to be married to feel good about yourself or to feel "whole," hold off. The first stage of any successful relationship, especially one that might lead to marriage, is successful separateness or successful aloneness: two people standing on their own two feet, fully capable of living without each other.

Are you whole enough yet to successfully live alone, facing your solitude? Have you worked through the very common despairing loneliness that follows divorce? In any marriage, much of one's self-identity comes from one's spouse. When that relationship is terminated, one's self-identity is dented if not destroyed. "If I'm not part of you, who am I?" But as one heals, one can see that aloneness and loneliness aren't the same thing.

In chapter 4, "How Did We Get Where We Are?" we looked at several codependent couples, one being Sally and Dave. Sally had grown up walking on eggshells, coping with an alcoholic father and she married Dave, whose anger she quickly excused. They divorced. What happened then? Here's the rest of the story.

At first Sally said she never wanted to marry again. But she was so lonely that when she met warm, caring Paul, she threw caution to the wind and fell in love—before she even knew he'd been divorced twice and was a recovering alcoholic.

As their relationship grew, Sally found out that Paul had a real temper, but, as with Dave, she made excuses for him, thinking she must have said the wrong thing at the wrong time. She started being oh so careful about what she said—walking on eggshells again and enabling his dysfunction.

Dear Sally was well on her way to a second disastrous marriage—because she was giving in to the desperate feeling that having someone was better than having no one. And that someone was very much like her first spouse—though she didn't see it as such. Codependency is blind—and perhaps one of the the primary reasons why second marriages fail.

Look at it this way: If you feel you don't really need to date, then it's probably time to consider stepping out. Generally, you're not ready to date if you've been divorced less than two years.

Beware if you're entering the dating (and potential marriage) scene looking for:

- financial security;
- sexual intimacy;
- a parent for your children—born or unborn;
- an escape from any imperfect living situation;
- an escape from personal isolation;
- a way to please your parents—or anyone else;
- a way to get even with your ex;
- a way to prove yourself desirable or lovable.

WHOM WILL YOU DATE?

If your answer is "Anybody who's warm and cuddly," hold off. You're dealing with short-term needs rather than with long-term goals. Consider these questions about your own values and standards:

- Do you have expectations as to how you will or will not be treated by a date? (This question is particularly important to someone who has been a victim of any sort.)

- Do you have spiritual standards for someone you will date? If so, what?
- Do you have educational, professional, or occupational standards for a date? If so, what?
- What sort of future community (church, denomination, social culture, political affiliation) do you want to be part of, and how will the individual you're dating lead you toward that community?
- Are you willing to compromise your religious convictions to date or marry?
- If you have or want children, what kind of a parent do you want for them?
- What kind of a spouse do you want—one who was like your ex or someone different? If different, in what way?

Here's a list of types of personalities that you're wise to steer clear of as you consider dating. They haven't worked through the deep needs that lead to codependent relationships.

The rescuer. This type of person is drawn to anyone who needs help. They bring home any "stray cat" or "lost puppy" that crosses their paths. They're great care givers. Unfortunately, they're usually also either dependent personalities or controllers, using the care-giving relationship as a mechanism for their own needs. Look at it this way: If you can't make it without being rescued, then the weight of your own emotional problems is eventually going to drown your partner. You don't need to be rescued. You need to be whole again. There is a difference.

The rebounder. This type of person seeks a level of intimacy and warmth within two weeks, or two months, that formerly took ten years to build. They are usually bouncing off of a failed relationship and will use you to attempt to replicate what was just lost.

It takes time to get over old hurts, and more time to build new and healthy support systems. People who try too quickly to duplicate what they just lost are living in denial. They haven't faced their own pain yet. Before they will be any good for another relationship, they need to grieve, forgive, heal, and successfully live alone for a while.

The one-upper. This person, still very angry and hurt regarding what happened in the previous marriage, ends up using people to fight back against the ex-mate. The attitude says, "I'll show him/her who can date around!" If you get involved with this person, you may find yourself being used and discarded, because you are merely a pawn in that person's battle with an ex-spouse.

Tip: *Anyone* who's still deeply angry, sad, hurt, fearful, etc., about almost anything at all, is a bad risk for marriage, for you will become the pawn in their battle with past ghosts.

Mr. or Ms. Independence. This person is the "rock," the "island." "I don't need anyone, and I never will." This is the person likely to say things like, "Once burned, twice shy," or, "I won't ever trust a man/woman again."

People like this are really saying that they have been hurt so badly that they can't trust anymore. They prefer to live within emotional shells, rather than risking real relationships. They attract "rescuers" like flies to honey. They make terrible choices for mates.

I've got to make up for lost time. This person is in a hurry to form a deep, long-lasting, intimate relationship. Perhaps her biological clock is ticking, and she wants children—soon. Perhaps he's terrified of aloneness and has been through so many failed relationships that he's trying too hard to make one work.

Just as when one encounters a salesperson who is trying to "close" the deal too quickly, it's usually wise to back away from this person. Otherwise you'll again become the pawn, as he or she works out old issues.

Tip: Good relationships, the ones worth building upon and sustaining for a lifetime, usually evolve over a period of time; risky ones frequently evolve quickly, with some sense of urgency.

The playboy/playgirl. If you want to keep out of anything real or potentially long-term just date a Barbie or Ken doll type. This "high maintenance" personality looks great but frequently has so many problems that honest intimacy and real commitment are out of the question.

Sometimes there's so much "ego" involved that there's no room for another person within the relationship. Sometimes there is serious personality disorder. This personality usually ends up using anyone to whom it attaches, and this usury always has negative effects upon one's self-esteem.

I'll take anything I can get. This is the "lost puppy dog" syndrome, almost always driven by severely low self-esteem, which destroys relational ability. A number of people may have tried to help "pump up" the low self-image, only to fail, and to leave the relationship frustrated.

Nobody can continually "pump up" someone who always needs to be pumped up. It has to come from within, and until that decision is made, it's usually a lost cause. Self-rejection frequently causes relational failure. Think of it this way: If one enters a relationship to pump up the other person and if the second person ever finally gets "up," will he or she need the first person any longer? Answer: frequently not.

The drifter. This person has been through several dating relationships and is generally not very well supported by same-sex relationships. This is the woman who knows how to look great and talk well, who comes on strong during the first few dates, or months, and then suddenly backs out of the relationship. It's the man who seems to have so much on the ball, who makes all the right moves initially, only to drop the ball suddenly when things start getting serious.

Tip: Do what physicians do when new patients come into their office—take a history. Find out a little about those whom you date. Do they date a lot? Ever been married before? How many times engaged? What are they looking for in dating?

I hope you find this list helpful—even as you look at your own readiness to date again. If you fit one of these categories, you need to work on your own "stuff" before you leap into new territory.

Divorced people are sometimes amazed at the number of "undesirables" who are immediately available and interested in dating. But consider this: How you communicate yourself to others will influence how people respond to you and what sort of people will be drawn to you.

If you are frequently pursued by people you can't stand,

stop and look at how you are communicating, especially nonverbally. Think about your overall appearance (manner of dress, hair style, weight, grooming); your social approach (eye contact, vocal volume and tone, flirtatious tendencies); manner of personal presentation (powerful, weak, needy, successful, in-control, out-of-control, happy, sad . . .). Social scientists estimate that 60 to 90 percent of all human communication is nonverbal. Look in the mirror. How are you projecting yourself?

AGE ISSUES

There's an old joke the punch line of which talks about a guy trading in his "old forty" for "two twenties." Divorced people often seek to marry someone significantly different in age, either significantly younger or significantly older. Either way it can be a red flag.

Divorced men often marry downward in age, finding a woman ten or fifteen years younger than themselves. Conversely, divorced women often marry upward, finding a man a few years older more comfortable than someone of equal age.

On the surface, males who marry down in age are frequently attracted to the more youthful appearance of the younger woman. At a deeper level, however, there is the issue of a younger woman being less difficult to impress and/or control than a peer. Younger women may respond more positively to the leadership (influence, control) of men who are a little older.

Females who marry up in age may be looking for economic security and sometimes a fatherly quality in a mate. As one individual quipped, "There's always something 'daddy-like' going on when there's a fifteen-year spread between her and him."

It's not always males who marry downward or females who marry upward. Sometimes following divorce males are searching for a mother figure to help make the pain go away. And sometimes divorcing females seek younger, more active, ener-getic men.

While there are always wonderful exceptions, in general, after divorce it's wise to date and marry within a four- to eight-year range of your own biological age. Although it's normal (and okay) to experience substantial swings in mood and attachment needs while going through divorce, as the pain fades (it will), your emotional age will once again likely reflect your biological age. If you marry someone outside your age range, down the road you may wonder how in the world you could have married someone so far removed in age, interest, and maturity level.

ISSUES OF SEXUAL ATTRACTION

There's no denying that sexual attraction and sexual needs are a real struggle for divorced adults. You've known and been known—in the biblical sense—and you no doubt ache in the absence of that physical intimacy.

But sexual involvement before marriage, though it meets short-term, immediate needs, tends to create distortions in the relational process and potential for incredible emotional pain. The closeness felt in the sexual encounter can be a counterfeit for true intimacy, which comes only through time and in the security of a committed relationship. Sex in this context is a quick fix for physical or emotional needs.

As for one's physical needs, our bodies were made so we can function without a partner. Some consider masturbation. Others rely on dreaming. The body will regulate itself.

As for emotional needs: Sexual release can be a way to temporarily avoid feeling the pain, aloneness, rejection, abandonment, or sadness of divorce. But the more sex is used to reduce or avoid emotional pain, the greater the probability that it will begin to dominate and control one's life and relationships. Recent research (*Contrary to Love: Healing the Sexual Addict*, by Patrick Carnes) demonstrates that sexual addiction is at least as difficult to break as heroin or alcohol addiction. How much wiser to learn to control and direct one's sexuality than to give it free rein.

Think of the sexual drive as being like a steam engine: It builds internal pressure, calling for release. If that steam-engine energy is simply released, the engine loses its power. On the other hand, if that energy is directed toward a purpose, the pressure can effect great feats—haul trainloads of coal, for instance.

Internal sexual pressure can provide substantial energy that you can use to effect your own healing and growth. For example, Harry meets Sally. They're both attracted to the other. They both want to make love. But they both know that it is in their best interest to save their sexual favors for their most intimate relationship, marriage.

So rather than making love, they use the sexual energy to fuel the relationship, to draw closer as good friends, to ask questions of each other, and to get to know each other deeply and intimately.

The sexual "pressure" that is there by virtue of their sexual natures is transferred into the "wheels" of the relationship—caring, affirming, communicating, trusting, and bonding. Premarital (or extramarital) release of that energy is almost always counterproductive to establishment and maintenance of intimate relationships.

Sexual activity in a relationship is never "neutral." It will build up or tear down a relationship. Those who use it as a toy, to use for gratification as needed, are most often the most damaged and relationally isolated—fearful and incapable of real intimacy.

Don't worry about sexual incompatibility. It doesn't exist. You don't need to build a sexual history but a relationship that can be trusted. A relationship that can't make it without sexual activity is at high risk for surviving the rigors of marriage.

In short, as challenging as it may prove to be, stay out of the bedroom and keep your hands away from sexual touching. With this standard in place, you will be able to use the healthy tension created by chastity to measure the depth and strength of your relationship.

Undoubtedly your divorce has forced you to think about your definitions of sexuality. In general, the more you define your sexuality in terms of orgasm, the more you will be controlled by your sexuality; the more you identify sexuality with orgasm, the more you will become a "thing" in search of another "thing" to help provide you with an orgasm.

Sexuality—your maleness or femaleness—is far larger, more beautiful, and more significant than an orgasm. Those who work toward enjoying their sexuality in nonsexually active ways are generally more at peace with God, with themselves, and with the world. They're also better candidates for long-term relationships.

Remember canoeing the white-water rapids? It's best to be prepared for what's ahead. This is especially important in setting sexual standards for yourself. Whatever values or standards you have, will be tested as you begin dating. Know where you stand and why, or you will find yourself sinking to the lowest common denominator. You will let your heart rule your head.

Sexual involvement appears to be the norm these days. Television and movies often present sexual activity as being SOP (Standard Operational Procedure), and that may be the way your date sees life. Know that maintaining a high standard may cost you the loss of a date.

If you choose to compromise your standards, you may end up resenting the person who led you to make the compromise. Besides that, clinical research is demonstrating that extramarital cohabitation has a negative impact upon marital success. No commitment (trial-basis relationships) means an open door to leave a relationship. Healthy people can commit; damaged people fear the word, preferring trial-basis relationships.

On the other hand, if you set your standards high, it may take you longer to make a connection, but you'll likely be more pleased with your decision in the long run.

Here are a few questions to ponder in regards to your sexual standards:

- How will you handle your sexual vulnerability when your hormones are running high, in the midst of a date, or after you've been dating for a few weeks or months?
- Are you willing to become sexually active to hold onto a relationship?
- What will control your decision making (in any area of the relationship), your emotions or your head?
- Given the variety of genitally transmitted diseases, what sort of sexual history will you ask of anyone you seriously consider for marriage? What medical information?

Standards and values will be tested. Count on it. Don't be dismayed, confused, or distracted when they are tested. Again, as you learn to walk close to God, you will find his wisdom leading you around many of the mine fields in the dating world.

MAKE DATING YOUR SECONDARY RELATIONAL SOURCE

Don't cut off your other relationships to give all your time to that special someone. Remember the trampoline support network? Those relationships—on all four sides of you—are vital to your continued health and stability. They're there to give you feedback and to balance your self-identity.

Maintain your nondating relationships as your primary network: parents, grandparents, children, siblings, uncles, aunts, same-sex friendships, co-workers, fellow church members, neighbors, and so forth. No one person can meet all your relational needs, and if you cut off your support, you and your date become an island—a needy and vulnerable island.

Mature relationships require time apart as well as time together. Don't forget the personal goals you've set for yourself. If you've determined to take one continuing ed course every semester at a nearby college, keep to your schedule. If you give one evening a week to volunteer work, continue sharing your talents. These activities are part of what make you whole—able to stand on your own two feet and contribute as an equal partner in a dating—or marriage—relationship.

And last but not least, don't ignore your relationship with God—the very core of your identity and your personal Rock of Gibraltar.

RECOGNIZE YOUR VULNERABILITY

Never underestimate the enduring impact of your divorce. Even if you take two or three years to heal and grow before dating again, you're still going to be somewhat vulnerable. Human beings were made for connection. Avoid making the mistake of ever believing that you are beyond the influence of your own vulnerability. Time and personal growth will lessen your vulnerability, but it's still going to be with you.

The closer you are to your divorce, the more vulnerable you will be, and the more prone you will be to making choices colored by your own immediate needs, that will satisfy those short-term needs but not satisfy anything for the long haul.

HOW TO JUDGE A DATING RELATIONSHIP

Any good relationship takes time to build. Like an oak tree, it grows slowly and steadily. It weathers storms, bends with the wind but doesn't crack. As you spend more time with someone, try to vary the circumstances. A formal dinner out followed by a movie doesn't provide you with insight as to how this person responds to other people or how well he or she communicates or deals with stress.

Review the chapter on communication and judge your relationship. Are you both able to talk freely about even difficult subjects? Does one of you monopolize the conversation or make all the decisions? Can both of you talk openly about yourselves? "Broken" people often "screen" realities—of their past or their feelings—from conversation.

As you try to judge the health of a relationship refer to the "Healthy Versus Codependent Relationships" list on pages 86–89 and the list below. Do you see codependent patterns starting to form in your relationship? Do you see patterns of your first marriage starting to repeat themselves?

No relationship will be perfect love—involving no infatuation. In the list below place a check beside each characteristic that applies to your relationship. Do the "loves" outnumber the "infatuations"?

Is It Love or Infatuation?

Characteristics of a Person in Love	Characteristics of an Infatuated Person
Is patient with all aspects of the relationship	Is impatient, with a sense of urgency ("Let's get *on* with this relationship!")

Characteristics of a Person in Love	Characteristics of an Infatuated Person
Is not jealous	Is often quite jealous
Is comfortable while apart from the other person	Is not comfortable apart
Exhibits little or no "emotional control" over the other partner	Exhibits high "emotional control" over other partner
Is responsible for one's own feelings and behaviors	Assumes responsibility for the other's feelings/behaviors
Shares feelings easily	Shares some feelings with difficulty
Is willing to give up short-term pleasures for long-term gains	Is not willing to forego short-term pleasures for long-term gains
Rarely thinks of the other person being "the ideal person" for me	Frequently thinks of the other person being "the ideal person"
Is able to let go, comfortably	Fears letting go
Gives, from sense of freedom and desire to share	Gives in order to get
Has personal sense of self-worth and self-esteem	Looks to the other for affirmation and worth
Is comfortable with flaws	Doesn't see the flaws; might not love if there were flaws

Characteristics of a Love Relationship	Characteristics of Infatuation
Is built upon trust	Is often built upon one or both partner's performance

Characteristics of a Love Relationship	Characteristics of Infatuation
Is based more upon friendship	Is based more upon need
Allows for independence and individuality	Seems to be all-consuming
Allows for both oneness with, and separateness from the other	Exhibits few, if any, "ego boundaries," i.e., "We are one." "We think and feel alike." "We know each other without knowing how we know."
Is based on high integrity	Lacks integrity (end justifies means)
Is based upon time and depth	Is based upon intensity and emotion
Is tested by time and variety	Is untested
Is stable	Is up and down, emotionally
Is committed "till death do us part"	Is focused more upon present moment, and "We'll see about the future when we get there"
Is based on open, comfortable communication	Is based on somewhat "screened" communication
Is based on mutual support and affirmation	Is based on need fulfillment

Cultural Definitions

You might analyze your relationship also by looking at a few common cultural definitions of love:

Love as Physical Attraction
Essence: Because you're handsome/beautiful, I love you.
Concern: Shallow definition; self-centered format; what happens if someone more attractive comes along or if normal aging erodes physical beauty?

Love as Emotional Feelings
Essence: Because I feel in love with you, I love you.
Concern: Feelings change.

Love as Fulfillment of Need
Essence: Because you meet my needs, I love you.
Concern: What happens if my needs change and you can't meet them; of if your needs change and I can't meet them?

Love as Giving
Essence: I give you all I have; therefore, you love me.
Concern: This is also a common way of controlling and manipulating. Giving is frequently a power play with obligations.

Love as "Mystical Connection"
Essence: You and I are one, cut out of the same cloth, soul mates, "meant to be" by some cosmic force.
Concern: Such great and deep connection usually reflects an equally great and deep need, which in turn reflects great and deep brokenness.
Essence: You are the only person in the world for me, and I am the only one in the world for you.
Concern: There is not a "one and only" person in the world for any individual. Most healthy people could have successful marriages with any number of healthy partners.

Grand Definition

Perhaps the grandest definition of love ever penned is found in the ancient Bible. It reads:

This love of which I speak is slow to lose patience—it looks for a way of being constructive. It is not possessive: it is neither anxious to impress nor does it cherish inflated ideas of its own importance.

Love has good manners and does not pursue selfish advantage. It is not touchy. It does not keep account of evil or gloat over the wickedness of other people. On the contrary, it is glad with all good men when truth prevails.

Love knows no limit to its endurance, no end to its trust, no fading of its hope; it can outlast anything. It is, in fact, the one thing that still stands when all else has fallen. (1 Cor. 13:4–8 PHILLIPS)

This is a good definition primarily because it's based upon healthy self-management and relational components. It leads to one final definition, again coming from the Bible and a Greek word, agape, pronounced "AH-gah-payee." The word for love has many connotations, including:

A decision—I will love you because I decide to love you.
A commitment—I will love you whether you deserve it or not.
A purpose—I will love you in a way that will make you a better person because I have loved you.
No exception clause—You can't make me stop loving you by anything you may do or not do, say or not say.
No time limit—I will love you forever.

Obviously, this is a tall order—at times far more than one could hope or ask, given our usual human selfishness. It's the type of love that God gives. It's the highest and best there is. The closer we can come to living it out, the better we are as human beings. There is one catch—this kind of love sometimes "costs" a lot. It's based upon a decision, not a feeling. It's there whether things are pleasant or terrible in the relationship. It's reliable under all circumstances.

Hard Questions

If you think you're in love, here are a few thoughts to ponder. Are you physically attracted to one another? Are you emotionally compatible? (Only time will tell you this.) Are you both mature enough to make a relationship work? Are you spiritually in tune? How wide is the age gap between you? Are you comfortable with each other's educational backgrounds, friends, social upbringing, values? Are you financially compatible?

Is the relationship primarily built around friendship or activities? If the former, great. If the latter, watch out, because activities can be a great way to avoid real connection.

If there are children, do they like both of you? If not, look out—step-kids can stress a second marriage faster and more profoundly than almost anything else, because they have the power to force one to decide upon love of children or love of mate.

How does it feel when you think of living with this person the rest of your life, every day? How does the word commitment feel to you? That's what wedding ceremonies are basically all about—commitment: "for better or worse, for richer or poorer, in sickness and in health . . ." Do you think you can make such a commitment? Can the one you're dating? What do both of your histories tell you about each others' abilities to sustain commitments? What have you done to walk away from the past codependencies?

MUST YOU DATE AGAIN?

Simple answer: You decide—and I mean you. Don't allow friends or relatives to push you into a dating relationship.

You do not have to date after divorce. There is nothing wrong with living your life without dating, if you so choose. In fact, in many cases it might be wise for you to date only very selectively.

If you do step out, realize this: *Ninety percent of first attempts at love, following divorce, fail.* You probably will not marry the first person you date or become infatuated with.

Take plenty of time to heal. Fill some of the loneliness with friendships and social involvements rather than with dating. Relax for a while. Unwind. Take a breather. Renew your walk with God. Grow spiritually. Rebuild your friendship network.

Gain some control in your life again. Actually, one of the worst things you could do for yourself is to rush into dating and marry quickly.

On the positive side, 80 percent of those who divorce eventually remarry. As you consider this, understand that those who do the best job of healing, who build solid and supportive networks of friends and become successful as single adults, have the best odds in making second marriages work.

Become that type of person. And if you date, date only that type of person.

QUESTIONS FOR REFLECTION

1. How do you respond to the thought that your personal, emotional survival depends upon you, not on some other person? How does this question bear upon divorce and dating issues?
2. How do you respond to the thought that you are at least partially responsible for the type of person who pursues you? Why is this true—or not true?
3. Reflect upon the section in this chapter dealing with love. How would you define the word? What criteria will you use to determine if you are in love?
4. It's important to deal with your own stuff before you start dating again. How is this possible, when we are so blind to so much of our own "stuff"?
5. How are codependent issues played out in the dating scene?
6. How important is it, really, to be successful as a single adult before attempting to reconnect via dating and marriage? What are some characteristics of a successfully single adult?

ACTION ITEMS

1. Take an evening this week, make yourself comfortable (perhaps with a cup of coffee or tea) in your favorite chair, and make a list of your own values in life. What

things are important to you? Why? (Refer to your personal-identity statement written in chapter 9.)

2. After you have made the list, place a star beside those items you would not be willing to compromise for the sake of a relationship.

3. Now imagine you are dating someone who is attempting to get you to compromise your values. What is your emotional response to that person? Write down your thoughts and feelings.

4. Make up a list of twenty characteristics of an individual you would consider marrying. After you've made the list, reorder it according to your personal values or priorities, with most important being at the top, and least important at the bottom.

FOR SPIRITUAL GROWTH

1. Return to page 215, and read 1 Corinthians 13:4–8. Make two lists—what love is and what love is not. Read your lists inserting the personal pronoun I in each characteristic: I am slow to lose patience. . . . I am not touchy, and so forth.

2. Read Proverbs 25:28. What does this verse have to say about dating?

3. In John 8:31–32, Christ promised freedom. What is the single condition he gave? How does this relate to your dating life?

4. Read Matthew 6:26–34. What does this teach regarding your present circumstances? Your approach to dating?

5. Read 1 Corinthians 10:13. What does this say about choices we make and how we justify our choices? How does this relate to dating?

People frequently make the mistake of thinking they can "do" marriage again, better than the last time around, by simply finding someone better than their ex.

Recently my wife and I had some problems with our new fancy cordless phone. It quit working, just quit. We took it back to the store and replaced it with a fancier one, with more bells and whistles. Now this new phone works, but it has a high-pitched buzz that is irritating. So today or tomorrow we'll take this one back and try yet another one.

Many people think marriage is like that. This one didn't work, so I'll go get another one. It's not that simple—not even close to being that simple.

‡

CHAPTER 12

CREATING HEALTHY MARRIAGES

At first I didn't even want to think about marrying again. It had hurt so badly the first time. As I healed, I once again began to want to marry.

When we first married, things were so wonderful. To be loved again was a joyful experience. But then the realities of a "blended family" began to set in, and since then it's been a joy, and a struggle too.

Most divorced people remarry. In *On Sex and Human Loving* Masters and Johnson say that 83 percent of men and 75 percent of women remarry. A common rule of thumb among therapists is that approximately 80 percent of divorced people remarry.

The statistical analysis of second or subsequent marriages varies somewhat and can depend on sex, age, race, educational background, and such variables. Yet remarriage stats are virtually never better than first marriage rates, and some stats demonstrate that second marriages could be profoundly more prone to fail than first marriages. Clinical research coming out of the University of Wisconsin suggests that second marriages may fail at a substantially higher rate (as much as 60 percent higher) than first marriages.

Second marriages are usually far more complex than first

marriages. Although each partner is older and one hopes wiser, each can be more damaged by the previous divorce. The legacy of the ex-spouse can continue to influence a new marriage. The financial picture can be more complex. If there are children, complex issues arise: step-parenting, visitation, financial child support, child discipline, varying children's allegiances, and on and on.

So if you are considering marrying a second time, don't expect it to be easier than it was the first time. It is doable, but it's usually tougher. The issues are potentially divisive. It's going to take more flexibility, more determination, more commitment, and more maturity. This is not all bad. It's just hard.

Considering the facts—that most people remarry and those marriages fail at a higher rate—the focus of this chapter will be to provide some information that can make second or subsequent marriages more healthy.

WALK WITH GOD

At the very beginning of their book, *Family Foundations*, Meier and Meier make an interesting statement. After citing the national average of fifty percent divorce rate, they address the divorce rates of couples who take seriously their spiritual growth and life:

> The statistics are much more encouraging here. Only one out of forty (2.5%) marriages of those who regularly attend church ends in divorce. And only one out of four hundred (.25%) marriages ends in divorce when the couple reads the Bible and prays together.

The point is clear: Spiritual growth is vital to marital success. Build your life on a spiritual foundation—two people walking and communing daily with God—and it's okay to "play the odds," because they're in your favor—four hundred to one.

> Delight yourself in the Lord,
> And He will give you the desires of your heart.
> Commit your way to the Lord,
> Trust also in Him, and He will do it.
>
> (Ps. 37:4–5 NASB)

Paraphrased and applied to marriage this text might read, "Delight yourself in the Lord, commit yourself and your marriage to him, and he will help you create the marriage you hope for." There's nothing mystical or magic about this. It's very basic, bedrock stuff. Like building a good house—start with a solid foundation, and then the walls and roof will fit smoothly.

Christ said the same thing in his Sermon on the Mount: "But seek first his kingdom and his righteousness, and all these things will be given to you as well" (Matt. 6:33). Begin your marriage with the best possible foundation.

MAINTAIN RIGHT PRIORITIES

My master's thesis project was based upon the idea that if one maintained certain priorities in 1-2-3-4 order, one's marriage would reflect high scores in marital quality in five areas: happiness, intimacy, stability, morality, and dependability.

The four priorities, in order, were (1) spiritual, (2) spouse, (3) children, (4) occupation.

The thesis project measured the effect on marriages when the four priorities were altered within marriage. That is, what would happen to the quality of a marriage when a couple placed their priorities in a different order? What would happen, for example, when a couple placed occupation as first priority—or children or spouse? What would happen when spiritual issues were last priority? And so on.

To measure the effect of these priorities, we surveyed a large pool, including both divorced and happily married people, suspecting that the happily married people would tend to rank their priorities 1, 2, 3, 4 (spiritual, spouse, children, occupation), and suspecting that the divorced people would tend to rank their priorities differently.

The findings were powerful (statistically significant at .01 level, for the reader who may know what that means). Basically, there was a strong correlation between maintaining those priorities in 1-2-3-4 order and high "marital quality" ratings. Marriages that put God first, spouse second, children third, and occupation fourth, tended to be happier, more intimate, more stable, holding higher moral standards, and more dependable than those marriages that ranked the priorities in some other order.

Second marriages frequently have a more difficult time maintaining these priorities in 1-2-3-4 order. If step-mother and step-daughter are having relational trouble, Dad may have to choose between child and spouse, seriously stressing the marriage. To handle stress, males frequently spend more time at the job, moving "occupation" into a higher priority than "spouse." To balance the stress, Mom may choose to draw closer to her own child of a previous marriage, moving "children" above "spouse" on the priority scale. And so it goes—downhill.

This set of priorities—spiritual, spouse, children, occupation, in *that* order—has been shown to work. We started this chapter by discussing the first priority—spiritual issues. Let's look at the others.

YOU AND YOUR SPOUSE

Happy, healthy marriages don't just happen. They are usually the products of very intentional and repetitive actions on the part of both spouses. Once either husband or wife begins to "coast," there's usually trouble ahead.

Marriages, like most human relationships, are frequently easier to grow while in their early stages, during the first year or two. Although there are always the "adjustment blues" as each party learns to fit in with the other, most marriages begin to face the most lethal enemy when one or both partners stops actively working at the relationship. As long as both spouses accept the responsibility that it is *their* marriage, *their* relationship, and are willing to do whatever it takes to build and mature it, they're usually fine.

The moment the relationship becomes a "secondary" or a neglected item, there's almost certainly going to be trouble. Healthy couples allow nothing to come between them. How?

BUILDING UP THE POSITIVE

As a general rule, it's far better to use one's resources to accelerate positive growth than to inhibit a negative habit. In counseling I've noticed that marriages in trouble are almost always stuck focusing their resources on the negative (usually found in the other person). One or both parties are trying to put out a fire, to fix the other person. Marriages humming happily along usually have two partners focusing their resources on what's good or right about each other, thereby fueling the right fire.

Two unique individuals will always find something in the other that is aggravating or abrasive. Nobody's perfect. There will always be things you wish to change in a mate, but the more you mature the more you realize that it's nearly impossible to change another person; it's difficult enough changing yourself. If change is in order, healthy marriages find the mates working at changing themselves, not their spouses.

Healthy marriages almost always find two individuals who work hard at *being* good mates—and that usually means two people who have trained themselves in the use of the compliment:

"You look great today, hon!"
"Thanks for keeping such a clean house."
"Thanks for taking me out on a date. I loved it."
"You're a good mother/father, darling."
"What a great meal! Thanks for your extra effort!"
"Thanks for washing the car for me. I was tired."
"Thanks for just holding me. I needed that tenderness."
"You still ring my chimes!"

You get the picture. Couples in marital trouble focus on catching each other "doing it wrong." Healthy relationships try to catch each other "doing it right" and build on the positive attributes.

Some couples have consciously built in a "ratio" of positive-to-negative reinforcement. Recognizing their tendency to notice what's wrong, they've decided to change the "climate" of their marriages by intentionally saying five (or eight or ten) good things to or about the another for every one negative thing they say. They know how important it is to fuel the right fire, to build upon what drew them together initially, and make sure that each partner knows he or she is appreciated and admired.

Philippians 4:8 supports this position: "Finally, brothers, whatever is true, whatever is noble, whatever is right, whatever is pure, whatever is lovely, whatever is admirable—if anything is excellent or praiseworthy—think about such things." Don't just think about them; talk about them.

Build Romance

You'll be surprised what this positive approach does to build romance, which is not necessarily sexual. Sure, there are times in which it's wonderful as husband and wife to have an evening of dinner and opera, followed by love making until the sun comes up. But most of romance is not that grandiose. Romance is best built upon small things—bringing home flowers for her now and then; a phone call at the office just to say, "I love you"; a nice long back rub with plenty of scented lotion; taking evening walks together holding hands—scheduling regular "dates" with each other. Healthy marriages recognize that romance is like a delicate flower: It takes frequent watering.

Communicate Openly

A healthy relationship with your spouse also relies on open and honest communication. Healthy marriages are those with few secrets—about personal history or personal feelings. Although there may be pieces of your individual history that you should not share, the fewer secrets there are, the less the marriage is compromised.

Marriage was created for companionship, and companionship is based upon knowledge and trust of one another. If someone truly loves you, unconditionally, there is nothing you can tell them about yourself that will cause them to change their love for you. The more open, trusting, honest, and vulnerable each partner is, the stronger the relational bond can be, the greater the depth of intimacy, and the more secure both partners can be in the fact that they know and are known, that they love and are loved.

Make Peace, Seek Peace

Couples with stable and healthy marriages usually have learned to seek peace. This doesn't mean they avoid dealing with real problems for the sake of peace. That is simply denial, repression, suppression, or avoidance.

Rather, the couples have placed relational harmony as one of their highest goals. Then when conflicts arise (as they always will), the goal is not winning the argument but resolving the conflict so that both individuals can again enjoy peace and love. Unhealthy relationships use conflict to win. Healthy relationships use conflict to strengthen the relationship and build peace and harmony.

This perspective is also supported by Scripture:

> Live together in harmony, live together in love, as though you had only one mind and one spirit between you. Never act from motives of rivalry or personal vanity, but in humility think more of one another than you do of yourselves. (Phil. 2:2–3 PHILLIPS)

Maintain a Statute of Limitations

One of the best ways to damage a relationship is to carry a grudge. The better one becomes at grudge retention, the more isolated one will eventually become. Why? Because *everyone* is *eventually* going to hurt you. Most of the time it will be by accident, but the pain will be real no matter what the motives.

Relationships need a "statute of limitations"—a point at which a person will choose to let go of any issue for the sake of the relationship. That point should be every day, when the sun goes down. Why carry yesterday's garbage into tomorrow? It's just going to smell worse tomorrow than it did today. Why ruin tomorrow?

Simply put: If it's a big enough issue to mention, do so today, talk it through, pray about it together as a couple, ask and offer forgiveness where needed, make any personal changes necessary, and resolve it. Then let it die an honorable death. Let it stay in the past where it belongs.

Scriptural support? "Never go to bed angry—don't give

the devil that sort of foothold" (Eph. 4:25 PHILLIPS). Even if you have to stay up all night to resolve the issue, do it. Learn to use God's statute of limitations.

Maintain Equality of Power

Dysfunctional marriages frequently find a severe imbalance of power: One partner controls all the money, or one makes all the major decisions. One always gets his or her way. One is considered to be scatter-brained by the other, or one is considered far more intellectually gifted.

Healthy marriages are built with equality of power, each spouse being as valuable, as relationally powerful, as important, as the other. Obviously, one partner may be physically stronger, one may be intellectually superior, one may make more money than the other, but there is still equality. One does not use the physical or intellectual strength, the money, or any other item, to push the other mate around.

Some Christians hold that the man is the "head of the home" and therefore granted the privilege of being a benevolent dictator. That perspective (usually based on Ephesians 5:22–24) is out of step with the balance of Scripture. Men who focus on that Ephesians 5 text should read verses 25–30, where Paul calls them to serve their wives as Christ served the church (sacrificial servanthood—not benevolent dictatorship).

This concept of a "balance of power" is clinical, found in text books, but it's also found in Scripture: "Submit to [be subject to, fit in with] one another in the fear [reverence or respect] of Christ" (Eph. 5:22, multiple versions blended: RSV, NASB, PHILLIPS). Healthy marriages are built upon peer relationships, equality, mutual respect, and balance of power.

FAMILY BEFORE WORK—OR POSSESSIONS

If you marry and have children—step-children or children of the new marriage—your spousal relationship should always come first. Husband and wife are going to need some time alone, away from the kids. Regularly building such times into your relationship is essential.

But a pitfall just as harmful as no time for the two of you will be having no time for family—including children. We live in what is probably the most materialistic culture of all history. Our comfort-oriented society tells us that success requires owning a Mercedes, living in a five-bedroom home in the suburbs, sending our children to expensive private schools, and buying clothes from Saks. People begin to value themselves by how much they are worth rather than by their relationships.

In the rush to accumulate things and generate enough money to support those things, people frequently get lost or trampled. Several years ago the dual-career family supplanted the single-career family as the statistically largest family grouping in America.

When the accumulation of things takes precedence over relationships with people, then people become means to get more things. Children get lost in this scramble. Marital partners grow distant, as friendship is replaced by newer toys. Relationships get compressed into encapsulated microwave attempts at "quality time." (Ever heard anyone say, "We don't have much time together, but what we have is real quality time?" Never believe it! It's impossible to compress such a lovely and delicate thing as a meaningful relationship into small bursts of intense, sometimes almost frenetic "quality time.")

Marriages that depend upon things to replace time and energy given to the family avoid the responsibilities of relationships. They create an end product that includes anger, emotional distance, and sadness. Without the family as a basis for self-identity and connectedness, children fall prey to a host of social and psychological illnesses.

The family is essential to individual security, identity, belonging, and communication of values; modeling is the primary way these values and identities are transmitted. To replace the family emphasis with success in accumulating things is not only selfish; it is also destructive to the growth and development of virtually every person in that system.

The challenge of the Christian family is not to find time, but to *make* it, and to make it ample enough to meet the needs of all family members. Job reward, whether it is money, power, authority, prestige, community leadership, spiritual leadership, or some other form of remuneration, must never replace the priority of family. The motto, "He wins who dies with the most toys," may be worthy of being called a joke, but it's not worthy of replacing family relationships.

BALANCE THE NEEDS OF PARTNER AND SELF

There is one more question to address: Where do I place "me" in that framework of priorities?

Healthy relationships allow for both self-development and nurturing of one's mate. Relationships in trouble frequently find one or both partners focusing almost exclusively upon their own needs, *or* the needs of the mate.

Again, a scriptural text may provide insight. When asked about the greatest commandment Christ answered,

> " 'Love the Lord your God with all your heart and with all your soul and with all your strength and with all your mind';
> and "Love your neighbor as yourself.' " (Luke 10:27)

The last five words provide the key to understanding appropriate self-care versus other-care: "Love your neighbor [or mate] as yourself."

Healthy people do not "lose" themselves within relationships with others. Healthy people give as much respect to their own dignity, their own values, and their own worth, as they give to others. Unhealthy people frequently demand or give too much. It is possible to "love too much," using the word love as Robin Norwood did in her book, *Women Who Love Too Much*. It is also possible to love too little, as when one is so focused on one's self that there is no room in the relationship for another person. Healthy marriages have good balance.

They also maintain the supportive networks—the trampoline—we talked about earlier. Marriages—as well as individuals—that isolate themselves almost always pay a heavy price for that isolation. For your self and your marriage, seek relationships based on health, support, and values, rather than on codependent need.

SECOND CHANCE

The most profound event in all human history was accomplished to provide a second chance. Christ, the Son of God, intervened in the midst of history to reconcile sinners to God. Second marriage can also be a second chance. It can be a time of healing, personal growth, maturing, and spiritual birth or recommitment. Perhaps the key issue in divorce, healing, dating, and remarriage has to do with one's personal decision regarding what to do with God's offer of pardon, healing, reconciliation, and new life.

It has been said that the kingdom of God is the kingdom of right relationships. Your ability to conduct right relationships is directly tied to your ability to walk with God. He is the map and the compass. Don't leave home without him.

QUESTIONS FOR REFLECTION

1. In your previous marriage, how did you rank the four priorities (spiritual, spouse, children, occupation)? How did your ex-spouse rank them? What impact did that ranking have on your overall relationship? What impact did that ranking have upon the happiness, intimacy, stability, morality, and dependability of your marriage?
2. Think about building and fueling relationships with positive affirmation. In your closest relationships, what do you think your ratio of positive-to-negative is? What affect has this ratio had on those relationships?
3. In your past marriage, how did romance and communication interact with each other? Was there a relationship between the two? If so, what was that relationship, and what can one learn about the two for use in future relationships?
4. How reasonable is it to have a "statute of limitations" within a marriage, especially in regard to significant issues that affect the relationship? What are the advantages/disadvantages?
5. How has materialism affected your relationships? How did it affect your previous marriage?

ACTION ITEMS

On a three-by-five card write out an outline of this chapter. Carry it with you. Practice specific pieces of this chapter in all your relationships. For example, try giving compliments or affirmation.

Use your three-by-five card as your own personal "relational score sheet," to see how well you are doing. Use the tools in this chapter not only in your friendly relationships, but also in relationships that are more difficult or painful.

For one month, keep a diary of your experience, which tools you used and how the tool worked for you. Review the diary from time to time to measure your own progress.

FOR SPIRITUAL GROWTH

Most of the major points in this chapter are based on specific biblical texts. Memorize these texts, making them your personal style of operation.

The more you are able to base any of your relationships on scriptural principles, the more smoothly they will work. If you find this to be untrue, assume that Scripture is correct, but your application of it may need adjustment.

If you have not yet done so, take the step of giving your life—lock, stock, and barrel—to the Lord. Invite him to become your Leader, your Lord and Master. Ask him to lead you to pieces of your life that need to be thrown out, cleaned up, or strengthened. As you sense his guidance, follow it.

If you don't have a Christian support and fellowship connection, create one. Find a church where you can get connected, where you can get spiritually "fed," and where you can also, in time, give back in service to others some of what God has given you.

If you've never done so, try spending regular time talking with God. You don't have to be good at it; God "speaks your language." For your own growth, use part of each day to connect with God—it's not for his benefit but for your own growth.

‡

APPENDIX: DEALING WITH ATTORNEYS

Selecting and working with an attorney can be one of the most trying aspects of divorce. Some attorneys are excellent; some are horrible. Some have good manners and treat their clients with respect; others have bad manners and treat their clients with disdain. Some are caring and supportive; others are greedy and manipulative. Some seek the least possible damage throughout the divorce process; others are willing to escalate the divorce proceedings to frightening heights of combativeness, hostility, and game playing.

You may already have an attorney with whom you are—or are not—pleased. We've included this appendix to help you understand the legal process and what you might expect as a result of that process. Knowledge can help you make wise decisions.

LEGAL APPROACHES TO DIVORCE

There are three basic approaches to the legal process of dissolving a marriage: (a) performing one's own divorce; (b) using a divorce mediator; (c) using a divorce attorney. Let's look at these three courses.

Performing One's Own Divorce

While this course is possible, it is usually not recommended and should be considered only in rare cases when:

1. The issues are relatively simple: no children; no real property; no self-employment or family business; low to moderate income levels.
2. There is no significant difference between spouses in emotional or legal power. The divorcing parties should feel equal in their abilities to read and understand their rights and obligations under the law. They must also feel equal in their ability to deal with the other spouse emotionally, without one spouse domineering, intimidating, or controlling.
3. Both parties must believe that divorce is the only option. If one party is intent upon saving the marriage, working jointly toward dissolution cannot be effective.
4. Both parties must be relatively free of strong emotions and able to work together without anger.

The basic advantage of performing one's own divorce is cost. In some states the only fee for such a divorce is the court filing fee, sometimes less than two hundred dollars.

A significant disadvantage is the time it takes to become familiar with divorce laws and court procedures. This factor and emotional-power issues often make this choice very challenging and difficult. If you start on this course and then have to hire an attorney in the middle of the process, your expenses can be higher than normal because of the items the attorney has to "straighten out." For this reason, in uncomplicated divorces some suggest hiring a young, less-experienced attorney who would provide necessary services at a lower cost than an attorney who has practiced for many years.

Think about it: If your situation meets the four requirements mentioned above and you're considering this route—if you are both emotionally stable, equally balanced in power, and cognitively capable of going through the somewhat complex paces necessary to handle your own divorce—it could be argued that you are probably capable of seeking professional help and rekindling your marriage.

Using a Divorce Mediator

In most major cities you can find professional divorce mediators who sit down with both parties of the conflict, listen to both sides, and then work out a solution that is (one hopes) suitable to both sides. In some cases the decision of a mediator is legally binding; in other cases it is not. The mediator does not represent one side or the other, but "sits in between" both parties, listens, asks questions, and generally helps the couple to resolve most or all of the difficult issues within divorce.

The process is simple, but, like negotiating one's own divorce, it is not a course to be taken by all divorcing parties. Some situations are too complex, and some marital relationships are too hostile and combative to be well served by a divorce mediator.

To consider using a mediator, both parties should believe that divorce is the only option, and both parties should be reasonably free of powerful emotions. Then, and only then, can the two divorcing individuals sit down together with a mediator and go over the difficult details inherent in termination of a marriage.

Most mediators will work with the couple to develop a workable agreement. Some recommend that the two spouses have the agreements reviewed independently by different attorneys, not so the attorneys can escalate hostilities, but so the agreements can be stated and structured within proper legal process. Once the agreement has been reviewed and mutually agreed upon, you can retain a less experienced (less expensive) attorney to process the agreement through the court system.

The primary benefit in using a mediator is cost. Mediators frequently charge less than half the hourly rate of an attorney. A secondary benefit is that mediators usually help the couple avoid the wild escalation and combativeness frequently inherent in the normal dual-attorney divorce proceedings.

The less complex the divorce, the more emotionally in control both parties are, the more equally balanced in power both parties are, the fewer real assets or properties, the more viable the services of a divorce mediator.

Divorce Attorney

Most couples struggling through the emotions of a divorce, complicated by property and custodial issues, will want to retain an attorney. The rest of this appendix will help you as you choose and deal with an attorney.

HOW TO CHOOSE AN ATTORNEY

First of all it's helpful for you to know the reputation of your spouse's attorney. As you know, some are highly combative, and others seek what is best and reasonable for their clients. Some specialize in divorce, while others have little experience in that arena. Knowing a little about the opposition can be helpful when positioning oneself for battle.

Seek Personal Recommendation

It's always helpful to know someone who knows and recommends the attorney. This allows you a chance to ask questions of style and reputation, and it is always appropriate to ask questions, many questions.

It is wise to know the nature of the relationship between the person giving the recommendation and the attorney. Does the recommending person work for the attorney? Is the recommender a close friend of the attorney? Is the recommender's opinion valid, or is it colored by some inside or special relationship?

Ask specific questions about fee structure and hourly cost. Does the attorney return phone calls? How much does he or she charge for receiving phone calls? Is the attorney aggressive? If so, how aggressive—to the point of being wildly combative or aggressive with reason and focus? Ask whether the attorney takes time to explain things, or just assumes that the client will go along with the recommendations made. How personable is the attorney? How genuine?

How well experienced? Is this his or her first divorce case? What's the attorney's win-loss record? Are there any pending actions against the attorney in the local state bar association? Any complaints to the Better Business Bureau?

Personally Interview Several Recommended Attorneys

Be very selective and thorough. A person can walk out of a divorce court with little or no money, little or no access to the children—tied to decisions that might look insane. Take your time in retaining an attorney. Don't just assume that the first to perform a dog-and-pony show is the best in town. After you've asked around, meet with a few attorneys. See how you interact with them. Ask every hard question you can think of.

Most attorneys will give clients a half-hour initial interview at no cost, but don't assume this to be true. Ask. When you meet with attorneys, tell them who has recommended them. Let them know that you're connected to other clients.

Don't give any attorney the name of others you're interviewing. Although it's contrary to good law practice to bad mouth the competition, attorneys are businesspersons trying to make a living by maintaining a corner of the market. Don't let them know who the competition is.

As you interview, ask about their divorce-practice experience. It's one thing to know divorce law. It's a far different thing to have a roster of satisfied clients. If there are any complications in your situation, don't go with a rookie. Seek a seasoned veteran.

Be very specific regarding fee structure. Working on an hourly basis, the minimum to expect in a large city is probably a thousand dollars, and this would be for a case involving no income, property, or custody issues. Obviously, the more complicated the situation, the higher the fee. Be wary of fixed-fee or low-cost divorces. The fee is often for paper work only, and phone calls, interviews, and so forth are all extra. Remember TANSTAFL—There Ain't No Such Thing As a Free Lunch.

Be fully prepared to explain your circumstances. Have your thoughts ready to present as clearly as you can. During the initial interview don't go into every sordid detail. Present an

238 | The Complete Divorce Recovery Handbook

accurate overview. If you decide to work with the attorney, details can follow.

Be prepared to listen carefully. Attorneys are people and occasionally give bad advice. If an attorney gives advice that contradicts your "better judgment," beware. If an attorney recommends something you know will inflame the situation between you and your spouse, ask questions: What's his or her motivation? Why is this being suggested? What will it accomplish?

At the end of this appendix you will find a lawyer-client questionnaire, which you might use as you interview prospective attorneys. At the close of the interview, you should be able to answer the following questions:

1. Does the attorney understand what you want? Does the attorney seem willing to help you achieve your objectives, or does the attorney seem to have a personal agenda—set of objectives and goals?
2. Do you have confidence in the attorney? Does it "feel" right? Remember, you'll be working very closely with this person, relaying deeply intimate details of your relationships and finances. You need to find someone you trust and with whom you feel comfortable.
3. Is the attorney professionally competent, well trained, and experienced in the ins-and-outs of divorce work? Don't go with a rookie.
4. Do you like the attorney's attitude, or do you feel belittled, patronized, or intimidated?
5. Are you comfortable with the attorney's level of aggressiveness? Hint: Most divorces are settled out of court. As a generalization, the more frequently an attorney goes to court, the more aggressive the personal style. Ask what percentages of divorces are settled out of court.
6. Does the attorney have a reasonable concern about fees? Are the charges unusually high? Does the attorney seem to be sensitive to your special financial circumstances?

WORKING WITH AN ATTORNEY

Here are a few do's and don'ts that are applicable to your relationship with your attorney. They may sound elementary. Even so, divorcing parties frequently and regretfully disregard them.

1. Don't get emotionally or sexually involved with your lawyer. People are particularly vulnerable at the time of divorce. Some attorneys take advantage of that vulnerability.
2. Don't use the attorney as your therapist. Stick to legal issues. Attorneys are usually well trained in the field of law; they are usually not trained at all in the fields of psychology or spiritual counseling. Use clergy, professional therapists, or close friends to work through the emotional and spiritual issues of your divorce.
3. Don't use a personal friend as your attorney. To be most effective your attorney needs to be emotionally objective.
4. Don't use your spouse's attorney or an attorney selected by your spouse.
5. Do consider waiting for emotions to subside before legally dissolving a marriage. Remember, time costs. You will be billed for each phone call.
6. Do have as much financial information put together as possible: salaries, other income, real estate, pensions, bank accounts, trust funds, investments, and so forth.
7. Do have some idea of what you want in terms of child custody, but retain your flexibility in this area. Remember, the more you escalate the conflict in this area, the more your children are likely to suffer because of it.

WHAT YOU MIGHT EXPECT FROM THE LEGAL PROCESS

Many people believe that the court system is biased in favor of the opposite sex, grossly unfair in terms of property distribution, and unfeeling when it comes to the welfare of innocent children. Welcome to the world of divorce law. Very few people leave the divorce court feeling that they "won." There are, in fact, no real winners in divorce proceedings.

If you're a man, you can probably expect to lose a major chunk of the financial base built during the marriage. You can expect that a mother's influence will carry greater weight than a father's. You can expect to pay child support until the kids are eighteen, possibly older if they go to college.

If you're a woman, you can expect your financial picture to change profoundly. You're not likely to get enough financial support to allow you to stay at home with the children. You'll probably have to earn a livelihood and pay for any child care out of your own earnings.

Either a divorce mediator or an attorney will probably try to work out an agreement similar to that which a court judge would grant. If you absolutely cannot come to an agreement out of court, you will be throwing yourself upon the "mercy" of the court, which means you'll have a judge (who wishes you would have settled out of court) making financial, child custody, and other decisions *for you*.

Most courts believe that a man's incentive must not be taken away. That is, a man shouldn't be so stripped of his earnings that he would lose a personal motivation to work. Because of this, settlements vary widely, depending on income levels of both spouses and accumulated property.

Each state has its own divorce law. Some states provide for alimony; some do not. Some states attempt to divide physical property fifty-fifty; others do not. Most states attempt to provide for child support of some kind, but again the laws vary widely.

When it comes to child custody, times are changing. There is almost no way to predict custodial outcomes. Some judges provide for split custody, fifty-fifty. Others provide legal custody to one parent but give broad visitation rights to the other. Some courts weigh toward maternal custody, but it's no longer the blanket "Mom gets the kids" that it used to be.

Again, remember that the kids are going to suffer far more than the parents in this battle. What's best for them?

Other possible areas of litigation:

- life insurance on wage earner for benefit of children;
- medical insurance for wife and children;
- cost of college for children;
- division of credit cards and credit histories;
- cost of dental and orthodontic work;
- division of cash, savings, checking, retirement funds, investments.

If at all possible, avoid litigation. Court battles will consume assets you are seeking to protect. The nastier each party makes the divorce, the more each side escalates to win, the longer the proceedings are dragged out, the more it's going to bust the piggy bank.

It is far better to seek professional therapy to help work through anger issues than to draw them into litigation and attempt to win in that arena. There are no winners in divorce court; people rarely leave the court room happy—no matter what the settlement.

To prepare for your own divorce proceedings (whether you settle in court or out), try to spend a day in divorce court, listening to other attorneys and couples going through the divorce process. The courts are usually open to the public. Go and become familiar with what your day in court could be like.

IS A CHRISTIAN ATTORNEY IMPORTANT?

Divorce by its very nature puts many people, including Christian attorneys, in difficult positions. For example, should a Christian attorney "go for the jugular vein" while representing a client? Should a Christian attorney allow a case to escalate until both parties are wildly out of control and the legal fees have built up until there is virtually no estate?

Some would argue that one facing a heart transplant should seek the best heart surgeon, whether or not the physician is a Christian. Others would argue that divorce is different, because moral issues potentially dominate many of the decisions; they feel a Christian attorney is important.

As in most matters, balance is critical. We would not recommend hiring an attorney simply because he or she claims to be a Christian. There are too many other questions to be answered, including professional competence and years of experience. There are also questions of faith: What does the word *Christian* mean to the attorney? Is it a marketing ploy used to attract a certain audience? Is it a matter of going to church once in a while and belonging to the "right" denomination? Or does the word *Christian* imply an allegiance to Christ, a strong moral character, honest and gentle interpersonal relational style, and a desire to live out the biblical messages of healing, reconciliation, forgiveness, patience, and humility?

If the former definition is used, there probably will be no substantive difference between working with a "Christian" or non-Christian attorney. If the latter definition is used, the attorney-client relationship will likely be richly improved—though this may have no bearing on the settlement you receive.

SHOULD YOU EVER CHANGE ATTORNEYS?

It is not at all unusual for individuals to change attorneys as they go through divorce. Some retain as many as four or five different attorneys. Usually, however, it's better to work with one attorney.

Increased cost is a primary factor. You usually must pay the first attorney's current bill before that firm will release your file to another. Then it usually costs money to retell all the stories, review the financial situation and the former attorney's progress, and bring the new attorney up to speed. Be sure it's worth the effort and cost involved in the decision.

From time to time a change in attorneys is appropriate. But before you consider firing your lawyer and hiring another, consider one point: Many, perhaps even most, attorneys consider divorce work to be messy, unenjoyable, not highly profitable, and quite stressful. Most attorneys don't wake up in the morning, stretch, and say, "Boy, I hope I get a real messy divorce case today!"

Consequently, many attorneys handle their divorce clients (consciously or unconsciously) somewhat differently than they might other clients, say a high-paying corporation. Face it, if you were an attorney and had two phone calls to return, one from a corporate vice-president whose business netted you fifteen thousand annually, and the other from an angry, bitter, emotionally demanding divorce client wanting basically some "venting" or "hand-holding" time, which would you return first?

This is not to say that your divorce case is unimportant to the attorney. It is, however, to put divorce cases in perspective, amidst the myriad other kinds of cases taken on by most attorneys.

Furthermore, each person has an individual management style and skill level. Some individuals are excellent managers, returning all phone calls within a half-day and monitoring all details with proficiency. Other individuals are more sloppy in people management and/or detail resolution. Attorneys are people too, and may secretly wish that messy and difficult (perhaps almost impossible to please) situations would just fade away. (Some may even unconsciously do—or not do—things to make them fade away.) Join the human race!

Certainly there are attorneys who simply don't care about people, who are interested only in money, and so forth. But they are the exception rather than the rule.

If you have a problem with the way you or your case is being handled, tell the attorney. Be forthright with your expectations and complaints. If phone calls aren't being returned, tell the attorney that you expect them to be. If you feel you're being treated unfairly or like a child, say what you think.

If you have a poor experience with your attorney, consider making a complaint to the Better Business Bureau. If you believe you have been treated in a grossly immoral or possibly criminal manner, consider making a complaint to the state bar association, which exists at least partially to police its members.

If, for whatever reason, you feel it's time to change attorneys, make careful and thoughtful—not rash or abrupt— decisions. Talk with others about your concerns. Do they agree with your assessment? Do they have thoughts as to how you might improve your relationship with your attorney?

In the final analysis, you have a right to change attorneys. Sometimes a change will be for the better, and sometimes you'll find you've jumped out of the frying pan and into the fire. If you decide to change, be at least as thorough in your selection as you were the first time.

Avoid jumping from one attorney to another simply because a friend tells you how her divorce settlement made her rich or really "got even" with an ex-spouse. Every divorce settlement is different. Just because someone else won a big settlement doesn't mean you will.

QUESTIONS FOR REFLECTION

1. If you have not yet chosen an attorney, list ten things that will be important in your selection.
2. Is it better to seek an attorney who will escalate and punish your ex-spouse or one who will seek to work toward a peaceable divorce?
3. What are the advantages and disadvantages of using recommendations from friends as you select an attorney?
4. Does an attorney's religious persuasion make him or her a better attorney? What "law" issues and "faith" issues might affect selection of and relationship with an attorney? Are they significant in the long run, in the "big picture" of divorce settlement?

ACTION ITEMS

1. Begin the process of getting referrals. Talk to friends. Call several attorneys' offices. Ask people who have been divorced. Get names of several attorney candidates.
2. Call the Better Business Bureau and see if there are complaints lodged against any of the attorneys you've selected. If so, consider the other names on your list.
3. Interview at least three attorneys.
4. Spend a day in court.
5. Spend at least a half-hour diligently praying about the selection you are about to make. Seek God's influence in the process.
6. Make your final selection.

FOR SPIRITUAL GROWTH

1. Read Luke 12:57–58. This passage deals with litigation, judges, and heated disagreement. What is the lesson to be learned? Does the lesson have any application in today's legal world?
2. Read Matthew 5:24 and Mark 11:25. What does this say about management of anger and holding on to (even legitimate) grudges?
3. Ex-spouses frequently become enemies. Scripture has a method of dealing with such people. Read Matthew 5:43–45. In your own words describe the method. Imagine how this would work in your specific situation.

LAWYER-CLIENT QUESTIONNAIRE

To make a reasonable and good choice in retaining a divorce attorney, you'll want answers to these general questions and issues. I've adapted this questionnaire from one which was given to me—unmarked, author unknown. I thank the anonymous author for his or her insight.

Name of attorney: _____

Address: _____

Phone: _____

1. Do you charge a straight hourly rate? If yes, how much do you charge per hour?
2. If you do not charge an hourly rate, how do you charge?
3. Are there any additional surcharges or bonus charges for service?
4. What is the smallest unit of time for which you will charge?
5. Do you charge for telephone calls to me or from me? Explain your telephone call policy and fees.
6. What is your estimate of the costs of my divorce?
7. What are the costs if the settlement goes to court litigation? Not all divorces go to court litigation—most are settled prior to court battles.

8. What percentage of your divorce cases go to court?
9. Will you give me a memo containing the pertinent facts of my case to be sure I have given you all the information you need?
10. In your estimation, how long will this divorce take—from [shortest time span] to [longest time span]?
11. How many custody cases have you litigated in court?
12. Are you going to be responsible for the tax advice in my divorce?
13. If you will not be, who will be responsible for this tax advice?
14. Will you communicate with my minister and/or my therapist? They should answer, "Yes, if *you* want me to do so."
15. If I want a meeting with you, the other attorney, my spouse, and me, will you arrange such a meeting?
16. As your office generates and receives letters and papers pertaining to this divorce, I would like a timely copy of each. Can that be arranged?
17. Upon my request would you send me your written *appraisal* of the major facts and issues of this case so that I may be made aware of them?

PERSONAL OBSERVATIONS AND COMMENTS

18. Overall personal warmth, genuineness, and apparent trustworthiness.
19. Overall apparent professional competence.
20. Any specific concerns regarding this attorney.
21. From whom did I obtain this attorney's name? Do I have a recommendation? Do any personal acquaintances know this attorney? If so, what do they say?

‡

NOTES

CHAPTER 3: STRESSED OUT!

1. The Lifestyle Profile was developed from a variety of scales. The Life Changes section is reprinted with permission from *Journal of Psychosomatic Research* 11, T. H. Holmes and R. H. Rahe, "The Social Readjustment Scale," copyright 1967, Pergamon Press, Ltd.

CHAPTER 5: WALKING THROUGH GUILT

1. S. B. Narramore, "Guilt: Christian Motivation or Neurotic Masochism," *Journal of Psychology and Theology* 2 (1974): 188.

CHAPTER 8: BUT CAN WE COMMUNICATE?

1. Sherod Miller, Phyllis Miller, Elam Nunnally, and Daniel Wackman, *Talking and Listening Together* (Littleton, Co.: Interpersonal Communication Programs, Inc., 1991). The Awareness Wheel is reprinted with permission. For more information on the Awareness Wheel and communication skills, materials, and programs, call 1-800-328-5099.

CHAPTER 9: GETTING YOUR ACT TOGETHER

1. Donald Joy, *Bonding* (Waco, Tex.: Word, 1985), 4.
2. Ibid, 6.

‡

FOR FURTHER READING

CHAPTER 1: GOOD GRIEF

Ahelm, Lloyd H. *How to Cope with Conflict, Crisis and Change.*
Jourard, Sidney. *Self-Disclosure.*
Kubler-Ross, Elisabeth. *Questions and Answers on Death and Dying.*
Landorf, Joyce. *Mourning Song.*
Lewis, C. S. *A Grief Observed.*
Lloyd-Jones, Martyn, D. *Spiritual Depression.*
Robinson, Haddon W. *Grief.*
Smoke, Jim. *Growing Through Divorce.*
Trafford, Abigail. *The Crazy Time.*
Wallerstein, J., and Blakeslee, S. *Second Chances.*
Westberg, Granger. *Good Grief.*

CHAPTER 2: FEELINGS: OH, WOE, WHOA, FEELINGS!

Dobson, James. *Emotions.*
Lloyd-Jones, Martyn, D. *Spiritual Depression.*
Minrith, Frank B., and Meier, Paul D. *Happiness Is a Choice.*
Missildine, W. Hugh. *Your Inner Child of the Past.*
Seamands, David. *Healing for Damaged Emotions.*
Swihart, Judson. *How to Live with Your Feelings.*
Tournier, Paul. *Guilt and Grace.*
Trafford, Abigail. *The Crazy Times.*

We strongly suggest you read Trafford's book if you're struggling with your own emotional roller-coaster ride.

CHAPTER 3: STRESSED OUT!

Colgrove, M., Bloomfield, H., and McWilliams, P. *How to Survive the Loss of a Love—58 Things to Do When There Is Nothing to Be Done.* (An excellent book—highly recommended.)

Fossum, M., and Mason, M. *Facing Shame.*

Glasser, William. *Take Effective Control of Your Life.*

Hershey, Terry. *Beginning Again.*

Jackson, Edgar. *Coping with the Crises in Your Life.*

McKay, Matthew, et al. *The Divorce Book.*

Marks, Issac. *Living with Fear.*

May, Rollo. *The Meaning of Anxiety.*

Ogilvie, Lloyd. *Making Stress Work for You.*

Sehnert, Keith. *Stress/Unstress.*

Smoke, Jim. *Growing Through Divorce.*

Weitzman, L. *The Divorce Revolution.*

CHAPTER 4: HOW DID WE GET WHERE WE ARE?

Beattie, Melodie. *Codependent No More.*

Berry, Carmen. *When Helping You Is Hurting Me.*

Black, Claudia. *It Will Never Happen to Me.*

Buhler, R. *Pain and Pretending.*

Forward, S. *Toxic Parents.*

Fossum, M., and Mason, M. *Facing Shame.*

Jordan, P., and Paul, M. *Do I Have to Give Up Me to Be Loved By You?*

Peck, M. Scott. *The Road Less Traveled.*

Rusk, Tom, and Read, Randy. *I Want to Change But I Don't Know How.*

Viorst, J. *Necessary Losses.*

Whitfield, C. *Healing the Child Within.*

Woititz, J. *Adult Children of Alcoholics.*

CHAPTER 5: WALKING THROUGH GUILT

Belgum, David. *Guilt: Where Religion and Psychology Meet.*

Fossum, M., and Mason, M. *Facing Shame.*

Jourard, Sidney M. *Self-Disclosure.*

Lewis, C. S. *A Grief Observed.*

McGee, R. *The Search for Significance.*

Missildine, W. H. *Your Inner Child of the Past.*

Powell, John. *Why Am I Afraid to Tell You Who I Am?*

Semands, David. *Healing Grace.*
Solomon, Charles. *The Rejection Syndrome.*
Tournier, Paul. *Guilt and Grace—A Psychological Study.*

CHAPTER 6: FACING FORGIVENESS

Augsburger, David. *Caring Enough to Forgive.*
Hershey, Terry. *Beginning Again.*
Smedes, Lewis. *Forgive and Forget.*
Smoke, Jim. *Growing Through Divorce.*
Towner, Jason. *Forgiveness Is for Giving.*
Walters, Richard. *Forgive and Be Free.*

CHAPTER 7: CHILDREN OF DIVORCE

Barnes, Robert. *Single Parenting.*
Berne, Patricia, and Savary, Louis. *Building Self-Esteem in Children.*
Berger, Stuart. *Divorce Without Victims.*
Bingham, Howard. *Living with Teens.*
Brenner, Avis. *Helping Children Cope with Stress.*
Campbell, Ross. *How to Really Love Your Child.*
Coleman, William. *What Children Need to Know When Parents Get Divorced.*
Ellison, Joanne, and Cataldo, Michael. *Raising Sons: Practical Strategies for Single Mothers.*
Faber, Adele, and Mazlish, Elaine. *How to Talk So Kids Will Listen; and Listen So Kids Will Talk.*
Faber, Adele, and Mazlish, Elaine. *Liberated Parents; Liberated Children.*
Francke, Linda Byrd. *Growing Up Divorced.*
Gardner, Richard. *The Boy's and Girl's Book About Divorce; The Boy's and Girl's Book About One-parent Families; The Parent's Book About Divorce.*
Gutley, Richard, and Koulack, David. *Single Fathers' Handbook.*
Hart, Archibald. *Children and Divorce: What to Expect; How to Help.*
Jewett, Claudia. *Helping Children Cope with Separation and Loss.*
Johnson, Margaret. *Divorce Is a Family Affair.*
Kersey, Katharine. *Helping Your Child Handle Stress.*
McFadden, Michael. *Bachelor Fatherhood.*
Maddox, Brenda. *The Half Parent.*
Miller, Kathy. *Out of Control.*
Peppler, Alice. *Single Again—This Time with Children.*

Phillips, Carolyn. *Our Family Got a Divorce.*

Quinn, P. *Cry Out!*

Reed, Bobbie. *I Didn't Plan to Be a Single Parent; Step-families Living in Christian Harmony.*

Rekers, George, and Swihart, Judson. *Making Up the Difference.*

Rodgers, Joann, and Cataldo, Michael. *Raising Sons.*

Smith, Virginia. *The Single Parent.*

Tickfer, Mildred. *Healing the Hurt.*

Vigeveno, H. S., and Claire, Anne. *Divorce and the Children.*

Wallerstein, Judith, and Blakeslee, Sandra. *Second Chances.*

Wallerstein, Judith, and Kelly, Joan. *Surviving the Breakup: How Children and Parents Cope with Divorce.*

Ward, Ted. *Values Begin at Home.*

Weiss, Robert. *Going It Alone.*

White, John. *Parents in Pain.*

Wilt, Joy. *Raising Your Children Toward Emotional and Spiritual Maturity.*

CHAPTER 8: BUT CAN WE COMMUNICATE?

Augsburger, David. *Caring Enough to Listen.*

Campman, Gary. *Hope for the Separated.*

Grand, Howard. *The Trauma of Transparency.*

Jourard, Sidney. *Self-Disclosure.*

Powell, John. *Why Am I Afraid to Tell You Who I Am?*

Sells, James. *Seven Steps to Effective Communication.*

CHAPTER 9: GETTING YOUR ACT TOGETHER

Berry, Carmen. *When Helping You Is Hurting Me.*

Buhler. *Pain and Pretending.*

Claerbaut, David. *Liberation from Loneliness.*

Fisher, Bruce. *Rebuilding When Your Relationship Ends.*

Hershey, Terry. *Intimacy: Where Do I Go to Find Love?*

Kennedy, Eugene. *If You Really Knew Me Would You Still Like Me?*

Newman & Berkowitz. *How to Be Your Own Best Friend.*

Osborne. *The Art of Understanding Yourself.*

MacDonald. *Ordering Your Private World.*

McGee. *The Search for Significance.*

McGinnis. *The Friendship Factor.*

McKay & Fanning. *Self-esteem.*

Rusk & Read. *I Want to Change But I Don't Know How.*

Semands. *Healing Grace.*
Solomon. *The Rejection Syndrome.*
Whitfield, Charles. *Healing the Child Within.*

CHAPTER 10: BIBLICAL PERSPECTIVES ON DIVORCE AND REMARRIAGE

Atkinson, David. *To Have and to Hold.*
Belovitch, Jeanne. *Making Remarriage Work.*
Duty, Guy. *Divorce and Remarriage.*
Ellisen, Stanley. *Divorce and Remarriage in the Church.*
Goldstein and Solnit. *Divorce and Your Child.*
Lovett, C. S. *The Compassionate Side of Divorce.*
McRoberts, Darlene. *Second Marriage.*
Medved, Diane. *The Case Against Divorce.*
Murray, John. *Divorce.* (Note, this book is somewhat technical.)
Plekker, Robert. *Divorce and the Christian.*
Purnell, Dick. *Free to Love Again.*
Richards, Larry. *Remarriage.*
Richmond, Gary. *The Divorce Decision.*
Small, Dwight. *The Right to Remarry.*
Small, Dwight. *Remarriage and God's Renewing Grace.*
Stott, John. "*Divorce.*"
Swindoll, Charles. *Divorce.*
Talley, Jim. *Reconcilable Differences.*
Woodson, Les. *Divorce and the Gospel of Grace.*

CHAPTER 11: DATING AFTER DIVORCE

Colman, Barry. *Sex and the Single Christian.*
Joy, Donald. *Bonding.*
Joy, Donald. *Rebonding.*
McDowell, Josh. *Givers, Takers, and Other Kinds of Lovers.*
McGinnis, Alan. *The Friendship Factor.*
Miles, Herbert. *Singles, Sex, and Marriage.*
Peck, M. Scott. *The Road Less Traveled.*
Purnell, Dick. *Free to Love Again.*
Short, Ray. *Sex, Dating, and Love.*
Swindoll, Lucy. *Wide My World, Narrow My Bed.*
Talley, Jim, and Reed, Bobbie. *Too Close, Too Soon.*
Tomczak, Larry. *Straightforward: Why Wait Till Marriage?*

Tournier, Paul. *Escape from Loneliness.*
Trobisch, Walter. *Living with Unfulfilled Desires.*
Trobisch, Walter, and Trobisch, Ingrid. *My Beautiful Feeling.*
Walter, Richard. *How to Be a Friend People Want to Be Friends With.*
White, John. *Eros Defined*
Wright, Norma, and Inmon, Marvin. *Dating, Waiting, and Choosing a Mate.*

CHAPTER 12: CREATING HEALTHY MARRIAGES

Achtemeier, Elizabeth. *The Committed Marriage.*
Christenson, Larry. *The Christian Family.*
Christenson, Larry, and Christenson, Nordis. *The Christian Couple.*
Dobson, James. *Love Must Be Tough, Straight Talk to Men and Their Wives, What Wives Wished Their Husbands Knew About Women.*
Evans, Louis. *Covenant to Care.*
Guernsey, Dennis. *Thoroughly Married.*
Joy, Donald. *Bonding.*
Kilgore, James. *Try Marriage Before Divorce.*
LaHaye, Tim. *How to Be Happy Though Married.*
LaHaye, Tim, and LaHaye, Beverly. *The Act of Marriage.*
Palmer, Earl. *Love Has Its Reasons.*
Rossman, Parker. *Family Survival.*
Smalley, Gary, and Scott, Steve. *For Better or For Best*; *If Only He Knew.*
Swindoll, Charles. *Strike the Original Match.*
Tournier, Paul. *To Understand Each Other.*
Trobisch, Walter. *I Married You.*
Wheat, Ed. *Love Life for Every Married Couple.*
Wiese, Bernard, and Steinmetz, Urban. *Everything You Need to Know to Stay Married and Like It.*
Wright, Norman. *Communication, Seasons of a Marriage.*

‡